Royal
Commission on the
Ancient and
Historical
Monuments of
Scotland

CW00554172

The Royal Commission on the Ancient and Historical
Monuments of Scotland gratefully acknowledges the
financial assistance of the following in the preparation
of this volume:

*Strathallan Pharmacy, Bridge of Allan, is pleased to support this
publication in the 150th year of its establishment.*

Clackmannanshire Council Museum and Heritage Service.

The Friends of Clackmannanshire Council Museum and Heritage Service.

Clackmannanshire Council Library Service.

SNOWIE

**The Snowie Group of Companies
- leaders in the waste management industry**

solutions today for a safer tomorrow

*the Forth
Naturalist
and Historian*

ISBN 9781902419251
© Crown Copyright 2008
Reprinted 2008

Royal
Commission on the
Ancient and
Historical
Monuments of
Scotland

'WELL SHELTERD & WATERED'
Menstrie Glen, a farming landscape near Stirling

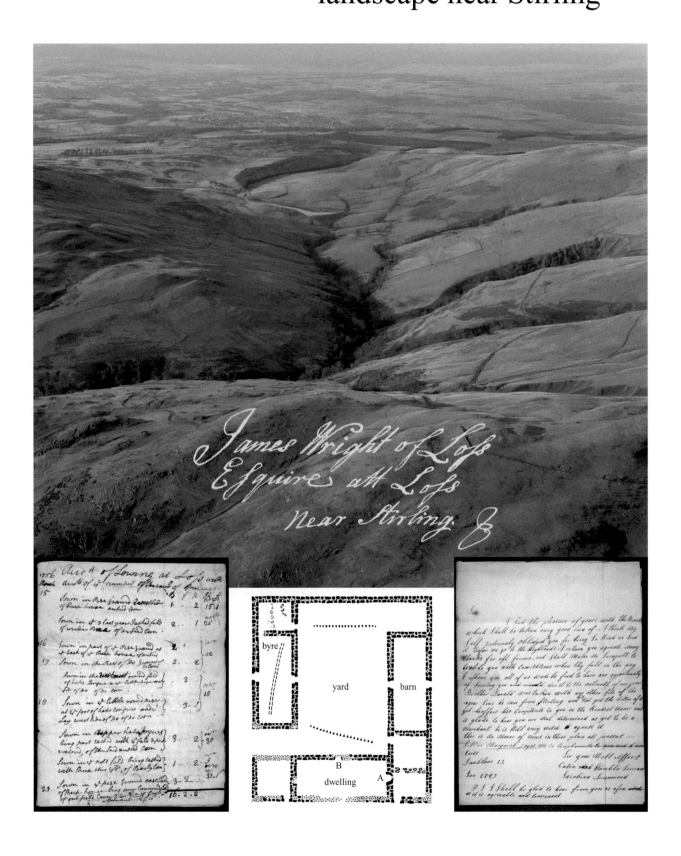

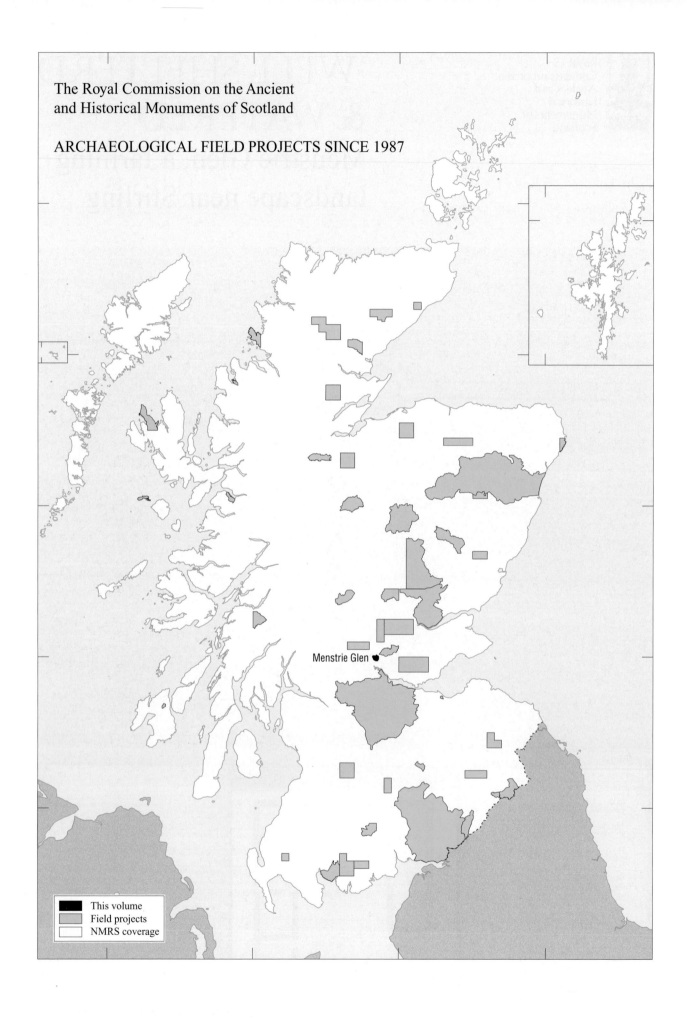

The Royal Commission on the Ancient
and Historical Monuments of Scotland

ARCHAEOLOGICAL FIELD PROJECTS SINCE 1987

Menstrie Glen

■ This volume
▨ Field projects
☐ NMRS coverage

TABLE OF CONTENTS

PREFACE

The title of this volume is taken from an advertisement for the tenancy of the farm of Lipney,[1] penned in 1760 by the landlord, as he took the first steps to the improvement of his estate in Menstrie Glen. Through his notes we glimpse the traditional farming landscape in the glen and the changes that he effected upon it. Landscapes such as this form one of the most extensive components of the archaeological record in Scotland, yet their physical remains have been little studied and are poorly understood. This study seeks to redress the balance, drawing as it does on the coincidence of visible archaeological remains and detailed historical sources. Similar landscapes are routinely revealed by archaeological survey, and equally detailed documents may occasionally survive in other archives, but their coincidence here is so rare as to be almost unique, providing insights into the evolution of the landscape and the interpretation of the field remains that are otherwise unobtainable.

The origins of this study lie with another happy coincidence, namely that of the interests of John Harrison, a private researcher based in Stirling, and the survey programme of the Royal Commission on the Ancient and Historical Monuments of Scotland. The Royal Commission, prompted by Historic Scotland, the Forestry Commission and Lorna Main of Stirling Council, set out to assess the extent and character of the surviving archaeological landscapes in the Ochils, where afforestation had already encroached upon large areas in the north-eastern half of the range. Aerial photographs taken immediately after World War II revealed the existence of extensive systems of rig-and-furrow, banks and enclosures (p.62, fig.57), but it was not known whether these remains still survived. Accordingly, two contrasting areas were targeted for fieldwork, the first covering Menstrie Glen at the west end of the Ochils, surveyed in 1997, and the second in Glen Devon, where work was undertaken in 1998.

Prior to the Royal Commission survey, private research by John Harrison had already identified the remarkable documentary material relating to Menstrie Glen that is contained within the Wright of Loss papers. These brilliantly illuminate the period from about 1750 to 1769, a time of fundamental change, not only in Menstrie Glen but also in the wider Scottish countryside. As such they offered an outstanding opportunity to combine the various sources in an analysis of the evolution of this landscape. Under contract to the Royal Commission, John Harrison has examined the available sources to provide the historical study that forms such a fundamental part of this volume.

The structure of the volume reflects the diversity of the source material, which is discussed in the Introduction. Beginning with sections on the history of farming and settlement, the main body of the volume provides a chronological discussion drawn from the documentary material. An analysis of the archaeological remains, introduced by studies of the patterns of land-use and settlement across three landscapes at Lipney, Loss and Little Jerah, is then followed by sections dealing with specific categories of monuments, including the evidence for mining. The volume ends with a short biographical sketch of James Wright, the key player in the creation of the landscape that survives today. Full references to the documentary material and published sources lie at the end, and are referred to in the text with a single sequence of numbers. There is also a glossary of terms at the end; this will be of particular assistance to readers unfamiliar with the old Scots terms found in the original sources, some of which are cited *in extenso*. Full results of the archaeological survey, including detailed site descriptions, photographs and plans, are available in the National Monuments Record of Scotland (NMRS). Site descriptions can be accessed through CANMORE at www.rcahms.gov.uk. The contents of the NMRS are indexed by 1:10,000 mapsheet, and the survey of Menstrie Glen falls on parts of NS 89 NW, NS 89 NE, NN 80 SW and NN 80 SE.

Fieldwork for the archaeological survey was carried out by G L Brown, D C Cowley, P McKeague, R Shaw and J B Stevenson, with the assistance of S D Boyle, M M Brown, P J Dixon, A Forster, A J Leith and G P Stell. The drawings and other illustrative work have been undertaken by G L Brown and R Shaw. Photographic services have been provided by R M Adam, T Duncan and D Smart.

The text has been written by D C Cowley and J G Harrison, with contributions from S P Halliday, and edited by S P Halliday and J B Stevenson. The layout of the volume has been prepared by J N Stevenson. The results of the survey have been incorporated into the National Monuments Record of Scotland by P McKeague.

The Royal Commission wishes to acknowledge the assistance given by the landowners, farmers and shepherds, who have allowed access for survey, namely Mr Burns, Mr MacLaren, Mr Mitchell and Northern Hydroseeding Ltd. Particular thanks are due to Mrs R Cowtan, for assistance with the documentary survey, Mr A Stirling of Keir, for permission to cite from the Stirling of Keir and Cadder papers, and S D Boyle, P J Dixon, R Tipping and G P Stell for advice in the field and in the preparation of the text. Thanks also to T H Ballantyne, Professor J Coles, L Corbett, K J Gray, D Hynd, L Main and S Mills.

Figures 5, 10, 15, 17, 33, 51A, 60, 61 and 62 are reproduced with the permission of the Keeper of the Records of Scotland. Figure 4 is reproduced by permission of the Trustees of the National Library of Scotland.

Menstrie Glen is in private ownership, and the intending visitor should seek permission for access locally. Great care is essential when visiting archaeological and historic monuments.

EDITORIAL NOTES

Text
Primary documents have been used extensively throughout the text, and quotations are indicated by the use of italics.

References
Bibliographic references are included in full in the Notes on pp.67-9 and as a consolidated list of published sources on p.70.
Documentary references: all manuscripts are referenced as Notes. The full reference in the endnotes is preceded by a three letter code to identify the location of the material. National Archives of Scotland – NAS; Glasgow City Archives – GCA; Registrar General for Scotland – RGS; Stirling Council Archives – SCA; National Library of Scotland – NLS. The Census Returns are held by the Registrar General for Scotland – though they are invariably consulted on microfilm.

Illustrations
Figure-captions: these have been prepared to explain and comment on the information the illustrations contain. Each incorporates appropriate site-names. Where a negative or original photograph material is held by the National Monuments Record of Scotland, the number of the scanned copy of the drawing or photograph in the archive is included (e.g. SC 584584).

Maps: each map is provided with a north point aligned on Grid North, and the National Grid is marked along the margins. The maps are based on information derived from various scales of Ordnance Survey maps with the permission of The Controller of Her Majesty's Stationery Office, © Crown Copyright, OS Licence number 100020548 2008.

Plans: surviving earthworks have been surveyed in the field, either by EDM or by plane table with self-reducing microptic alidade. The depiction of cultivation remains on plans is heavily reliant on features visible on aerial photographs, in particular where they are barely visible on the ground. A legend to the conventions that have been employed at scales of 1:250 and 1:500 is provided below.

wall (above sill level)	wall (below sill level)	core	line of wall	bedded stones	stones	bank	ditch	scarp

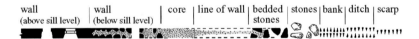

Fig.1 This oblique aerial view of Menstrie Glen from the south, shows Menstrie village in the foreground, and the hills rising up to the watershed to the rear. The aerial perspective has flattened the dramatic escarpment along the south face of the hills. SC 579498

INTRODUCTION

Menstrie Glen is one of a number of valleys that break through the jagged façade of the escarpment forming the southern face of the Ochils. The village of Menstrie itself stands on the low-lying ground at the mouth of the glen, where the deeply incised Menstrie Burn debouches from the hills onto the lowlands, draining into the River Devon near its confluence with the Forth. The sides of the glen rise steeply to a series of interconnected rounded spurs framing the skyline on the north and east, while the rocky boss of Dumyat forms its western side. Rising so dramatically from the Forth Valley, the escarpment affords spectacular views to the south, an amenity highlighted in an advertisement for a farm in the glen written as long ago as 1760 (fig.5): *'the house of Lipney is pleasantly situated upon ye south side of the hill, immediately above the low grounds from whence there is a very fine commanding prospect of a beautyfull country and the River of fforth'*.[2]

The topography of the glen has had an enduring impact on the pattern of land-use and settlement. The watercourses are deeply incised, creating natural barriers that have conditioned the division of the land, while a broad terrace, which extends around the valley sides, has provided the focus for cultivation and settlement. The steeper slopes above this terrace in turn give way to the hill tops, which have always provided the bulk of the rough grazing. Stands of trees clothe the banks of the burns, protected from the predations of grazing beasts by the steepness of the slopes.

Using the historical sources it has proved possible to trace the expansion and contraction of settlement within this topographic frame over a period of about five centuries, from several medieval sheep farms to the densely settled and farmed landscape that existed in the first half of the 18th century. Thereafter the glen was effectively cleared and turned back to sheep. Today, it is a very empty place, unpopulated but for the sheep, and frequented only by shepherds and hillwalkers. In this human desolation lies its interest to the

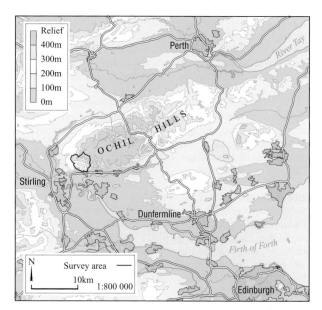

Fig.2 Map showing the location of Menstrie Glen at the western end of the Ochil Hills.

landscape historian, for the relatively low intensity of land-use over the last 200 years has preserved the earlier settlement pattern relatively unscathed. Not only do the farms with their buildings and yards survive, but also their fields and enclosures. The bare bones of this sketch do little justice to the patterns and processes that emerge from the archaeological and documentary surveys. The latter in particular reveals the human agencies that have produced the present-day landscape of the glen, which is as much a product of management as the intensively farmed lowlands below the Ochils escarpment.

Fig.3 This ground view looks southwards down Menstrie Glen to the valley of the Forth. The broad sloping terrace upon which the majority of the cultivation and settlement remains are found is clearly visible in the foreground and on the opposite hillside, and one of the deeply incised watercourses that divide up the glen can be seen on the right. SC 579492

SOURCE MATERIAL

Before examining the history of farming and settlement in detail, it is important to consider the sources of information that are available, if only to understand their limitations. As has been suggested, the historical and archaeological evidence complement each other, but both are only partial records, and neither provides a uniform level of information for each of the main periods of occupation that have been identified. Nevertheless, the documentary sources reveal the processes and, in some cases, the agencies of change, while the mapping of the archaeological features illustrates the spatial and morphological patterns at various stages in the evolution of land-use and settlement.

Documentary sources

Published material on land-use and settlement in the western Ochils over the last five centuries is limited. The three editions of the *Statistical Accounts* provide contemporary glimpses into land-use patterns at the end of the 18th century, in the mid-19th century, and after World War II,[3] while a history of Logie Parish by Menzies Fergusson includes a review of land ownership since the medieval period.[4] More recently a survey of place-names in the Ochils has drawn on maps, plans and other manuscript sources.[5] Few other writers have explored the manuscript sources for the Ochils, and the detailed documentary material examined in this publication has only been collated as a result of the search by John Harrison. The availability of source material and the detail recorded in it is variable. There is no documentation earlier than the 15th century, and it is scanty for the period up to the end of the 17th century. The 18th century is well-documented, in particular the period between about 1750 and 1769, but thereafter manuscript sources are scarcer. Paradoxically, the more recent periods of land-use, in the 19th and 20th centuries, are very poorly documented.

In addition to these books and manuscripts, maps created from the mid-18th century are another important source of information for settlement and land-use. The production of maps, however, is not driven by the requirements of future landscape historians, and the depiction of features is directly related to the purposes for which they were drawn. For this reason the presence or absence of farms and settlements on maps cannot necessarily be taken as a reliable guide to their occupation or abandonment at a particular date. No clearer illustration of this exists than General Roy's map of Scotland, surveyed between 1747 and 1755.[6] It depicts the Menstrie Burn running back into the hills but does not show any settlements or cultivation. And yet, the evidence that will be advanced in this volume will show that the glen was teaming with activity at this time. James Stobie's map of 1783 (fig.4) raises other problems.[7] It depicts Jerah, Ashentrool, Loss, Ploverburn and Backside and Foreside of Lipney, indicating that there were buildings standing at these locations in the 1780s. Not all were tenanted farms, however, and it is likely that the map does not represent the totality of settlement in the glen at that date, nor does it make any attempt to depict the extent of cultivation. In contrast, the omission of Backside from Morrison's map of 1848 is a good indication that this farm had been abandoned by that date.[8] Indeed, if the lack of documentation is any guide, it had been long abandoned by then. With the advent of Ordnance Survey mapping in the mid-19th century, the criteria for the inclusion of features on maps became more explicit. The depiction of roofed and unroofed buildings, and the disposition of enclosures around them, can be taken as an accurate rendition of what was in use when the survey was undertaken. However, the depiction of relict landscape features, such as the substantial head-dykes in the glen, was evidently not considered important.

The principal unpublished sources that have been consulted fall into three main categories – the Wright of Loss papers,

testaments, and tacks and rentals. In addition, there are a number of minor sources that are considered separately below.

Wright of Loss papers
James Wright of Loss (p.64) owned half of Menstrie Glen during the mid-18th century. He was an obsessive note taker and hoarded paperwork relating to his lands and business interests. His papers, held as an uncatalogued collection in the National Archives of Scotland (RH15/115/1-5), are the single richest source for the glen. The papers include some 17th-century material, but most of them were generated between 1750 and his death in 1769. During that time Wright farmed Loss, his small estate at the head of the glen. Lipney, his adjacent property, taking in the east flank of Dumyat, was leased to tenants. From 1761, he also rented Fossachie, which lies to the west of the survey area (fig.12), from the Airthrey estate. This was a crucial period of change in the glen, and his papers provide a rare insight into the processes that were in operation. On a broader canvas, the papers record his livestock dealing business, which ranged from the Western Isles to London.

Testaments
Testaments list (or purport to list) the assets and liabilities of a person at the time of death. In the 17th century they took the form of a complete list of livestock, grains and other produce, of rent owed, and of other details of the social context of the deceased and their families. Those dating from the 18th century tend to be less detailed. Collectively, however, they give a fairly cohesive picture of farming and social standing, which can be used to good effect in reconstructing changing farming practice.[9] There are 30 testaments for people who lived in and around Menstrie Glen between 1605 and 1700. A good example of one of the 17th-century testaments is that of Thomas Henderson, tenant in Jerah, who died in April 1687. He had an old horse, five cows, three bullocks and 35 sheep (including ten ewes and ten lambs). That spring he had sown 7 bolls of outfield oats and $1^{1}/_{2}$ bolls of infield oats, each expected to yield a threefold increase, and he had $1^{3}/_{4}$ bolls of barley in his barn. His two employees were owed wages and he also owed the landlord rent for this and the previous year.[10]

Tacks and rentals
Thirty-nine tacks relating to fifteen sites in and around the glen have been gleaned from estate papers (Wright of Loss, Elphinstone of Airth and Stirling of Keir) and from the various Registers of Deeds (see *Other papers* below). They range in date from 1660 to 1813, the majority lying between 1720 and 1760, and vary considerably in the detail they provide. Nevertheless, tacks reflect broader patterns in farming and land-use practices. They allow rough estimates of the size of holdings to be made from rents, and also provide specific details that are invaluable for the reconstruction of landscape history. For example, a tack of Foreside and Quarterside of Lipney of 1740 defines the marches of the grazing by reference to points which can still be identified on the ground today (p.46).[11] In other cases, details of grazing practices are mentioned, such as 'loanings' for the herding of cattle. Some tacks place limits upon the activities of tenants, such as those granted in 1742 and 1743 by the Keir Estate for Ashentrool, Longcraig, Cauldhame and Whittetsbank, which forbade the keeping of sheep.[12]

Other papers
In addition to the three main categories of material that have been examined, a number of other sources have proved useful, namely papers relating to neighbouring estates, census returns, and other minor local records. The Stirling of Keir and Elphinstone of Airth estate papers (Glasgow City Archives and National Archives of Scotland respectively), for example,

do not rival the rich detail of the Wright collection, but they extend the documentary record of settlement in the glen into the early 19th century. The Registers of Deeds of the Sheriff and Commissary Courts of Stirling and of Dunblane (all four are in the National Archives of Scotland) also yielded some items, including several tacks and a Decreet of Division, while census returns record a phase of abandonment beginning by 1841. The latter also give occupations of the inhabitants, which provide some clues to land-use in the glen in the mid-19th century. Finally, Logie Kirk Session Minutes, Stirling Burgh Records and other local sources (mainly in Stirling Council Archives) provide incidental information.

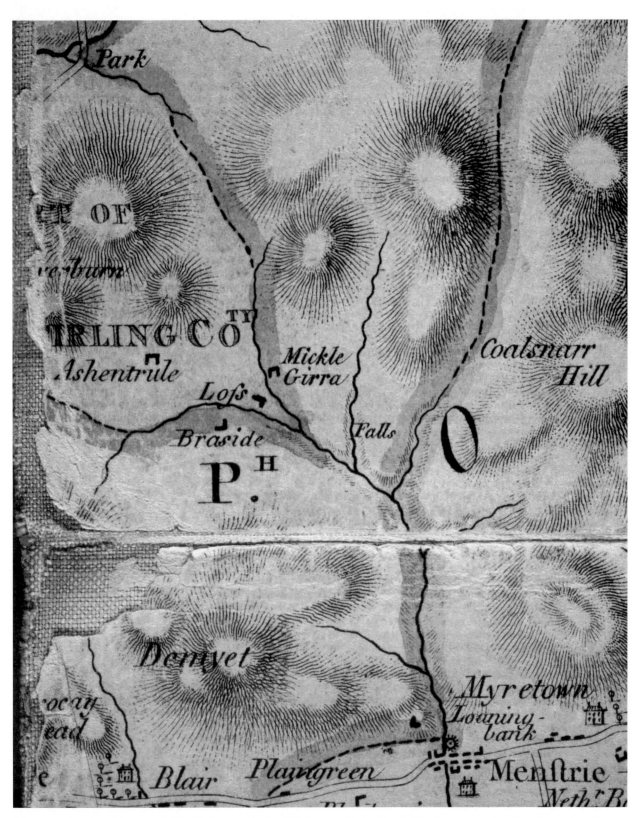

Fig.4 Extract from James Stobie's map (1783) of the Counties of Perth and Clackmannan, showing Menstrie Glen. County maps such as this tend not to show all the occupied settlements and make no attempt to depict the extent of the agricultural land. Reproduced by permission of the Trustees of the National Library of Scotland.

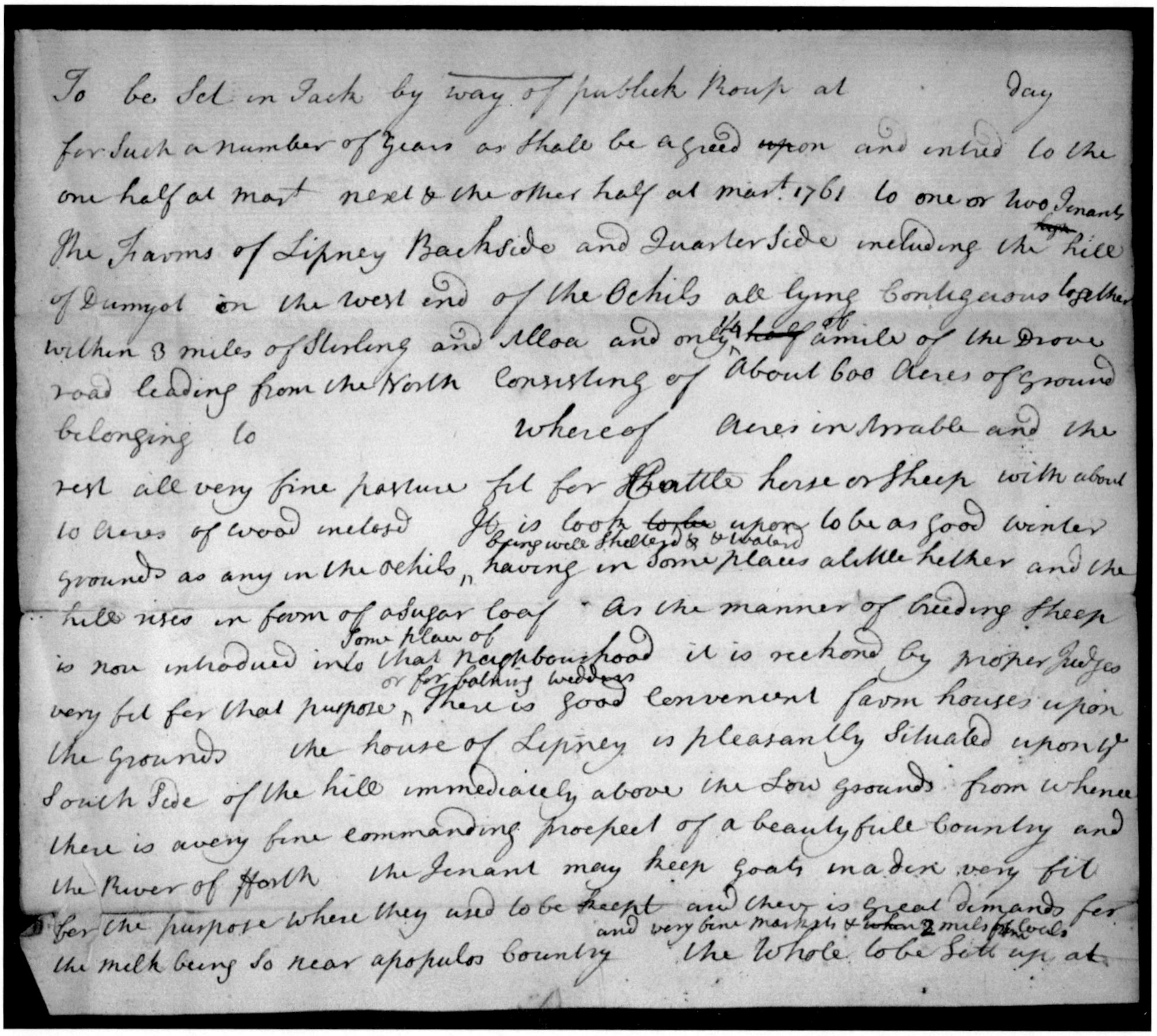

To be set in tack by way of publick roup at   day
for Such a number of years as shall be agreed upon and entred to the
one half at Mart(inmas) next & the other half at Mart(inmas) 1761 to one or two tenants
the Farms of Lipney Backside and Quarterside including the hill
of Dumyat on the West end of the Ochils all lying Contiguous together
within 3 miles of Stirling and Alloa and only ¼ half of a mile of the Drove
road leading from the North consisting of about 600 Acres of Ground
belonging to   whereof   Acres in Arable and the
rest all very fine pasture fit for Cattle horse or Sheep with about
10 acres of wood inclosed It is look to be upon to be as good Winter
ground as any in the ochils being well shelterd & watered having in some places a little hether and the
hill rises in the form of a sugar loaf. As the manner of breeding Sheep
is now introduced into some plan of that neighbourhood it is reckoned by proper judges
very fit for that purpose or for fatning wedders There is good convenient farm houses upon
the grounds   the house of Lipney is pleasantly situated upon ye
South Side of the hill immediately above the low ground from whence
there is a very fine commanding prospect of a beatyfull Country and
the River of fforth   the Tenant may keep Goats in a den very fit
for the purpose where they used to be keept and there is Great demand for
the milk being so near a populos Country and very fine markets & when 2 miles from Coals the whole to be sett up at

Fig.5   This page and opposite. This draft of the advertisement for Lipney written in 1760 on both sides of a single sheet of paper is taken from the remarkable collection of papers and notes amassed by James Wright of Loss in the mid-18th century. Reproduced by permission of the Keeper of the Records of Scotland (NAS, RH15/115/3/2, Bundle B).

at £50 of yearly Rent
        (the Articles & Conditions of Roup)
for further particulars inquire of the proprietor at Loss who will
Show the Grounds and treat with any about a private bargain
Letters adressed to the care of the Post master of Stirling will come safe

                reserve parks.   And Backside Crofts & Drum
            reserve Liberty to inclose & subdivide & them to pay ½ per cent
            reserve from Subletting to the Dausons & and not to graze
                                any but what leaves ye Dung upon ye ground
            cause Houses be repaired & Quarterside houses built
             reserve Parks & backside ye length of Stonehill & Liberty
             for Cows to goe to muir in winter

Archaeological survey

The field survey of the glen was undertaken by small teams of Royal Commission archaeological survey staff. Electronic Distance Measurement (EDM) equipment (fig.6) was used to plot each structure and bank against the detail of the modern OS map. Some areas of cultivation remains that were not closely defined by banks or other mapped features were also plotted on the ground; the remainder have been mapped from aerial photographs. The more ephemeral remains of cultivation are frequently difficult to see in the tussocky grass, and in many cases have been slighted by recent improvement. Fortunately, the RAF vertical photographs taken immediately after World War II, were flown under ideal conditions, with oblique sunlight striking many of the hillsides at low angles. This has served to bring many of the cultivated areas into high relief, providing an immediate indication of the character of the remains. In other areas the photographic cover has been supplemented with oblique views taken in the course of the Royal Commission's own aerial survey programme. The dimensions and characteristics of each structure within the survey area were recorded in the field into a database on a hand-held computer. This record was used to produce summary site descriptions for the NMRS, and, together with the survey data and photographs, form a project archive that is available for public consultation.

The nature of the archaeological record

The survival of visible archaeological remains of any age is conditioned by the extent and intensity of subsequent phases of activity. This general rule is particularly apt for agricultural activity, which, mainly through cultivation, involves processes of destruction, remodelling and over-printing that obliterate redundant features from earlier patterns of use. Consequently, in such a landscape the archaeological remains form a mosaic from which discrete phases of land-use can rarely be disentangled in their entirety. This poses a considerable problem for any correlation between the visible features in the landscape and the complex processes of land-use and change evident from historical documentation. At best these are only hinted at in the surviving field remains. Where change can be identified on the ground, it often represents only the major episodes of reorganisation, such as the building of march-dykes or the abandonment of an area of arable, rather than the ongoing activity of the farming cycle (but see p.42).

Menstrie Glen is no exception to these rules, and the surviving archaeological remains throughout the Ochils are heavily biased towards those reflecting the latest stages of medieval and later land-use and settlement. A thin scatter of earlier monuments attests to a human presence in the Ochils since the Mesolithic period but, with only two possible prehistoric monuments in Menstrie Glen, a standing stone and a dun, it is difficult to gauge the extent of settlement before the medieval period. The former stands on the line of a trackway crossing a knoll low down on the east flank of Dumyat, and may not in fact be of prehistoric date; the latter, set back from the mouth of the glen on the west flank of Myreton Hill, is one of a small number of minor fortifications in the Forth valley of late Iron Age or early medieval date. Although some of the buildings and the clusters of shieling-huts recorded during the survey may be of medieval date, cultivation in the 17th and 18th centuries has effectively removed any trace of a wider pattern of permanent settlement and land-use dating from before 1600. On the other hand, with the creation of large sheepwalks in the second half of the 18th century, the extent of arable diminished rapidly, and there has been little subsequent cultivation or any other form of destructive land-use in the glen. This has ensured the survival of much of the 17th- and 18th-century landscape, whereas arable agriculture in adjacent lowland areas has continued apace, erasing all traces of earlier features not compatible with large, regular fields.

Variations in the patterns of survival are not the only factors influencing the character and distribution of archaeological records held in local and national databases. The intensity and type of survey, for instance, vary enormously across the country and have a measurable impact. This is illustrated to good effect in Menstrie Glen, where the recent Royal Commission survey noted 87 sites, of which 80 (92%) were mapped and placed on record with full descriptions for the first time. Of the several known prior to the present survey, variously recorded in the 1960s and 1970s, three were discovered by the Archaeology Division of the Ordnance Survey, three by private individuals, and one in the course of earlier Royal Commission work. These gave few clues to the richness of the landscape that has been revealed by the present survey.

Fig.6 Archaeological survey in progress – the Electronic Distance Measurement equipment seen here ensured that the metrical accuracy of the survey was maintained throughout the glen. SC 579496

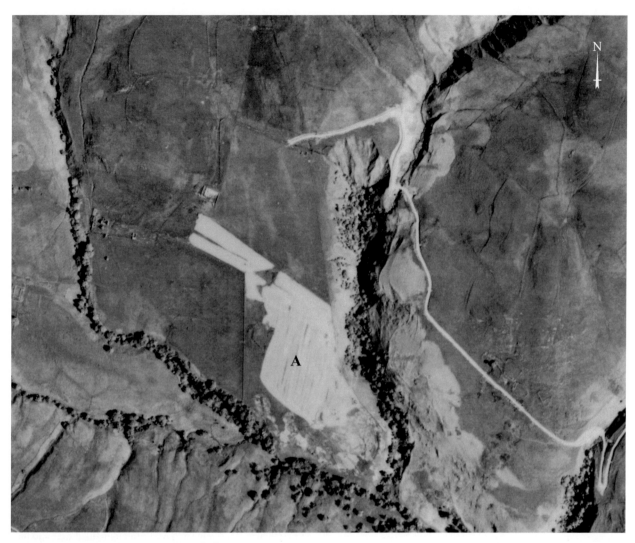

Fig.7 The contraction of cultivation after 1760 has lead to the preservation of large areas of the pre improvement landscape. A few of the fields have continued to be ploughed from time to time, however, such as those seen in this vertical aerial view of Jerah, captured while liming was in progress (A) on 10th June 1988. All Scotland Survey. SC 579485

Fig.8 View across Menstrie Glen to the rough grazing on the north flank of Dumyat, with one of two coniferous plantations in the glen in the foreground. SC 611368

THE HISTORY OF FARMING IN MENSTRIE GLEN

The fragmentary nature of the historical sources for the glen before the 17th century is matched by that of the archaeological record. Thereafter, however, an increasingly detailed picture is revealed by the manuscripts, culminating in Wright's papers covering agricultural improvements in the mid-18th century. At the same time, there is a corresponding increase in the quality of the archaeological record.

The first part of this chapter deals with the evidence of the farming landscape in the period from 1450 to about 1600, and the second with the pattern of landholding that emerged at the beginning of the 17th century. The third and fourth sections provide an overview of the broad evolution of farming practice and the patterns of management of the landscape between 1600 and 1750. The fifth section discusses Menstrie Glen on the eve of the improvement period, as seen through the eyes of James Wright, and is followed by a brief description of the emparked landscape he created around his house at Loss. The final section details the changes that took place with the improvements after 1760 and the subsequent development of farming.

The late medieval period 1450-1600

During the medieval period the greater part of Menstrie Glen was Crown land, as was the whole of the western end of the Ochils. The lands of Menstrie, on the east side of the glen, had come into the possession of the Campbells of Argyll by the early 14th century,[13] and the neighbouring property of Jerah, in the heart of the glen, was in the hands of the Cistercians of Culross, remaining under their control until at least the 1530s. The Crown lands in the western part of the glen were divided into three holdings – Lossintrule, Lipney and Fossachie.

The boundaries of these five holdings are difficult to reconstruct with complete confidence, but several clues are provided by the old county boundaries that cut idiosyncratically across the glen. Lossintrule, for instance,

probably corresponds with a portion of Stirlingshire (fig.9) that was detached from the main body of the county until 1899.[14] To the east, this area marched with Perthshire along the Crunie Burn, a fairly well-defined topographical feature that may be reasonably postulated as the march between the medieval holdings of Lossintrule and Jerah. The eastern extent of Jerah can be defined likewise, marked by the county boundary between Perthshire and Clackmannanshire, which followed the line of the Second Inchna Burn.[15] This burn flows through one of the steep-sided gullies that form the natural boundaries on the east side of the glen. To the east and south of Jerah lay the lands of Menstrie. The boundaries on the western side of the glen are not so well-defined topographically, but the county boundary between Perthshire and the detached portion of Stirlingshire follows the Loss Burn, and this probably corresponds to the march of Lossintrule with Fossachie and Lipney.

The five properties thus defined provide the overall framework of the landscape that emerges in 1450. Fossachie and Lipney extended out of the glen on the south and west, taking in the whole of Dumyat, while Jerah and Lossintrule similarly extended over the watershed on the north and east. The Menstrie Estate held the south-eastern parts of the glen (Inchney and Myreton), with its centre lying on the carseland at the foot of the escarpment to the south. The centres for Fossachie and Lipney may also have lain elsewhere on their holdings, the latter perhaps in the vicinity of the unlocated chapel of Lipnoch recorded at the beginning of the 16th century.[16] Only the foci for Jerah and Lossintrule lay within the glen itself. The lands of Jerah and Lossintrule differ from those of the other three properties in being entirely upland holdings. This may reflect some aspect of the subdivision of the Crown holdings during the medieval period.

Between 1450 and 1500, those holdings belonging to the Crown appear to have been largely given over to pasture and were grazed by sheep. This pattern of use probably extended to Jerah also, and seems to have been maintained well into the 16th century. A tack of 1534 for Jerah to Margaret Bonkhill granted woods, plains, meadows, pastures, hawking, hunting, fishing and common pasture (fig.10); all categories clearly indicating that the majority of the open ground was still in pasture.[17] A subtack of 1538 by Margaret Bonkhill to James Porterfield and John King granted the right to occupy the land with their own goods (usually meaning livestock, but not precluding arable) or to lease it to tenants.[18] These various sources do not deny the existence of some arable ground before the early 17th century but, on balance, it is likely that the glen was primarily a sheep pasture from at least the 15th century. The subtack also indicates that in some parts of the glen a hierarchy of tenants was probably established by the early 16th century.

During the late-15th and 16th centuries ownership of the glen was changing. By 1480 Fossachie was '*in the hands of the laird of Luss*', but by 1510 it had passed to George Shaw, remaining in the possession of the Shaws of Knockhill for most of the 16th century.[19] By 1510 Robert Callander of Manor (on the carseland beside the Forth) had a charter of Lipney and Lossentrool.[20] And by 1526 the earls of Argyll had granted a charter of their lands of Menstrie, which included parts of the eastern slopes of the glen, to Andrew Alexander, whose family were to hold it until about 1640.[21] Despite these changes, the integrity of the properties themselves appears to have been maintained into the 17th century.

Landholding and farm organisation 1600-1750

The mechanisms that saw ownership passing to local lairds during the late-15th and 16th century are by no means fully understood. Nevertheless, there can be no dispute that by the 17th century the glen was occupied largely by tenanted farms,

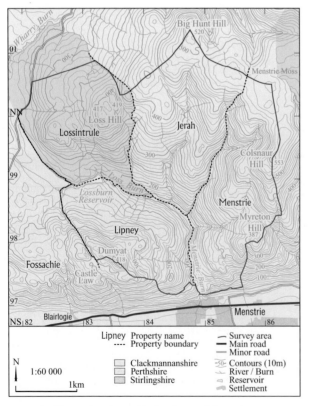

Fig.9 The old county boundaries of Stirlingshire, Perthshire and Clackmannanshire have probably preserved elements of the medieval property boundaries in Menstrie Glen.

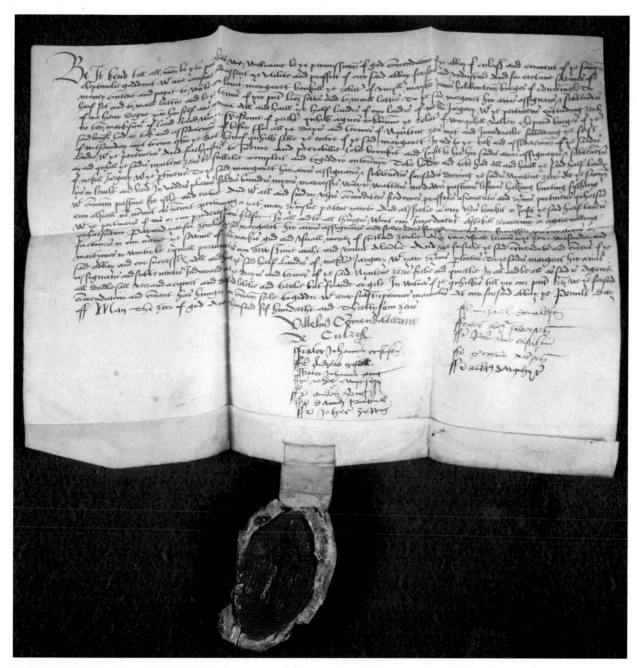

Fig.10 This tack of 1534 to Margaret Bonkhill indicates that most of the ground on Jerah was still in pasture in the early 16th century. Reproduced by permission of the Keeper of the Records of Scotland (NAS, GD 124/17/188).

a process that may have been initiated by the transfer of ownership. The exceptions were Lipney, which was, for a time, owner-occupied, and Fossachie, where the character of the tenure of the Duncansons is not clear. At precisely what date these farmsteads were first established is not recorded, but only for Lipney and Jerah is there any evidence for a medieval date. Thus, following the transfer of ownership, probably during the mid- to late-16th century, the large sheepwalks of the medieval properties were divided into a pattern of small farms, practising a mixed arable and pastoral economy.

The main period for which there is detailed evidence for landholding and farm organisation is the 18th century, although many of the patterns evident in this material are likely to have belonged in the 17th century. The disposition and size of farms are likely to have been conditioned by the deeply incised watercourses that divide up the natural landscape of the glen. Nevertheless, estate and farm boundaries were not rigid and there was considerable flexibility in the organisation of the

tenancies. Joint tenancy, a widespread arrangement for leasing farms in Scotland, was also a feature of holdings in Menstrie Glen. Donald McFarlane and Andrew Roy, for example, took a joint tenancy of Lipney in 1730; in 1732 they divided it into two distinct tenancies, namely Foreside and Backside, but the grazing above the head-dyke was still shared.[22] Later still, in 1752, McFarlane and Roy shared the White Meadow and the Greens of Craigneish; they were allowed to plough half each, but if they did not plough it the pasture was to be shared.[23]

It was not only the lands of the holdings that were intermixed in this way. The boundaries of the estates were equally complex. This is most clearly seen in the north-west of the glen. There, in 1762, Cauldhame was owned equally by Wright and his neighbour, Keir, on the north and west, with their tenants' lands in runrig. A similar arrangement had existed for Lossinrule before it was divided, giving Ashentrool, Longcraig and Whittetsbank to Keir, and Loss, Ploverburn and Callendar to Wright. That this division had not

17

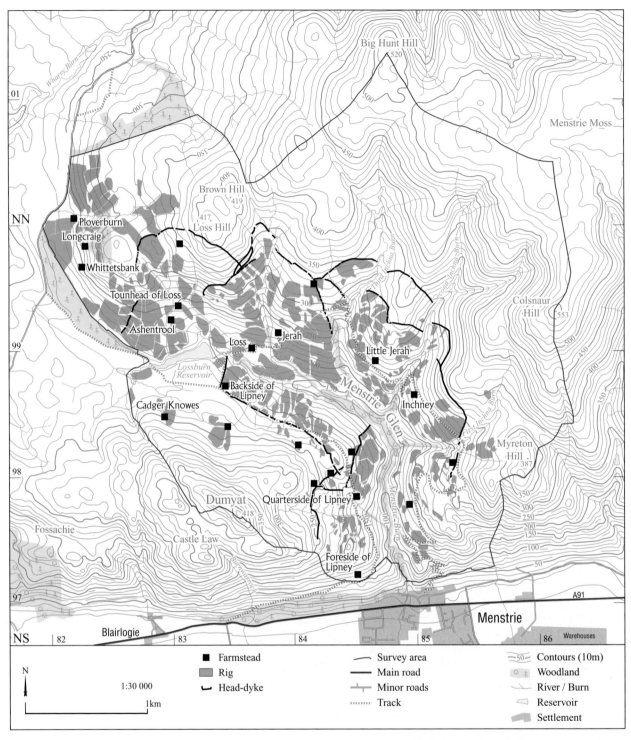

Fig.11 This map shows the dense distribution of settlements in the glen dating from before the reorganization of the landscape in the 1760s. These are set against the patterrn of head-dykes and the maximum extent of cultivated ground.

created geographically discrete units is evident in a Contract of Division and Excambion dated 6th April 1762; this records: '*Yet the marches above the houses of Ashentrool are irregular and partly contraverted. And besides, the high ground thereof called Ballochill has still remained undivided and the saids other farms of Longcraig, Whittetsbank, Ploverburn and Callander are much scattered and interspersed* (with one another and with Cauldhame)*, which is inconvenient for labouring, inclosure and improvement*'.[24] The tone of this document echoes the feelings of many Improvers commenting on pre-improvement arrangements,[25] and underlines their desire to rationalise landholdings into the geographically distinct units characteristic of more modern landholdings.

Farm units before the improvements were evidently not of a uniform size. About 1761 Loss had 25 acres of infield,

including the garden, 66 acres of outfield interspersed with grass, 71 acres of hill and pasture ground, and the right to half of the 52 acres of the Common Hill. In contrast Cauldhame had only 10 acres of infield, Ploverburn 11 acres, Whittetsbank 7 acres, Longcraig 7 acres, and Ashentrool 12 acres; these shared 138 acres of grazing on the Common Hill.[26] The variations in the sizes of the farms are also clear from the rentals.[27] This can be seen, for instance, in the new tacks raised by the Keir estate to all the tenants of their part of Lossintrule in 1742 and 1743; the cash component of the rent was £34 each for Whittetsbank and Longcraig, and £67 for Cauldhame, with other duties in proportion.[28]

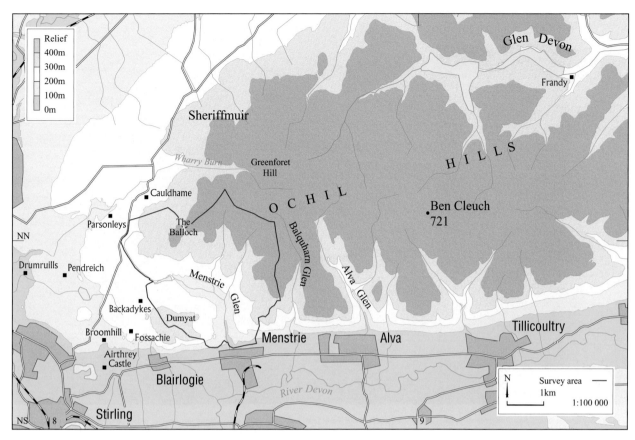

Fig.12 This map of the western end of the Ochils shows the locations of sites referred to in the text.

The evolution of the farming landscape 1600-1750

The conventional view of settlement and farming during the 17th century has been one of stagnation preceding the great flowering of the Improvements in the 18th century. Commentators of the 18th century, however, had a vested interest in promulgating a view of agriculture in the previous century as inefficient and backward, if only to highlight the benefits of improvement. This view finds resonance in some of the mid-18th-century documentation from Menstrie (below). However, in his study of 17th-century agriculture in Scotland, Ian Whyte has demonstrated that this is a misrepresentation of a period during which changes and developments were set in train that were to have a fundamental impact on the subsequent century.[29] Innovations such as liming were in place in some parts of the lowlands during the first half of the 17th century, and a programme of legislation by Parliament between 1661 and 1695 encouraged landowners to experiment with new crop rotations, livestock breeding and woodland management. Enclosure and other improvements remained on a small-scale, but their presence warns against a simplistic view of events during the 17th century. What cannot be disputed is that the pace of change increased after 1700, and in the middle decades of the 18th century a whole-scale transformation of land-use took place.

The assessment of the farming practices in Menstrie Glen is complicated by its topographical position between the Highlands and the Lowlands. Both are likely to have cast their influence over the area. In the Highlands cattle-rearing dominated, while in the Lowlands the emphasis was on arable farming. This further complicates the assessment of what changes were afoot before detailed documentation becomes available in the mid-18th century. A study by Harrison of agriculture in Falkirk Parish between about 1600 and 1720 has shown that even within quite small areas there was considerable potential for variation in the patterns of land-use.[30] He identified four broad zones, ranging from 'traditional' farming on the higher ground, to progressive, market-orientated farming on the low ground, with transitional

areas lying between them. The differences in the pattern extended beyond variations in the natural productivity of the land itself, reflecting also the sizes of holdings and the capital available for investment. Menstrie Glen, lying adjacent to lowland areas and Stirling on the one hand, and beside a major droveway from the Highlands to Falkirk on the other, shares many of the characteristics of the transitional areas of Falkirk Parish. Farms were of modest size, and the ratios of oats to barley tended to be about 5:1, rather than the 10:1 found in the upland parts of Falkirk. Legumes, prominent features of the heavily capitalised coastal fringe of Falkirk Parish, are rarely found in the glen, and wheat is entirely absent from the records.

The transformation of Menstrie Glen from a sheep walk at the end of the medieval period to a patchwork of mixed farms by the 17th century was undoubtedly a complex process, of which the documents provide only the broadest outline. Some sequence in the establishment of the farm units is probably indicated by the location of the earliest of the documented settlements in what may be described as primary locations, generally on south- or east-facing slopes. A pattern of subsequent expansion and infilling by later and smaller farm units is evident in their position in less attractive spots. For example, by the beginning of the 18th century Lipney was divided into Foreside, Quarterside and Backside, of which Foreside, lying on the south-facing slope at the mouth of the glen, is the primary farm (see pp.45-7). In addition to Quarterside and Backside, the archaeological survey has revealed at least six undocumented byre-houses, probably the foci of small farm units, scattered across the same area. Although these farmsteads are possibly part of the late-17th-century pattern of settlement, they are more likely to have been the settlements of subtenants or cottars dating from the 18th century. It is notable that all of these farmsteads lie in less favourable locations, in three cases on north-facing slopes in the shadow of Dumyat. A clearer indication of this sequence in the establishment of the settlements is documented in 1627. In that year Lipney and Fossachie both paid some grain as

Fig.13   The topographical position of Menstrie Glen at the boundary between the hills and the lowlands can be seen in this oblique aerial view looking eastwards along the south face of the Ochil escarpment, which rises abruptly from the carseland beside the River Forth. Menstrie lies above and to the left of the Wallace Monument, which is in the centre of the picture. SC 579457

Fig.14   This vertical aerial photograph of an area on the north flank of Dumyat shows traces of small scale arable intakes of common grazings lying beyond the head-dykes, some of which are probably those referred to tacks and rentals (A,B). Backside of Lipney (C) and part of the adjacent head-dyke lie bottom left in the picture. (106G/SCOT/UK120, 20 June 1946, 3048). SC 579465

20

teind, and Jerah paid 260 merks money, 18 stone of butter and 9 bolls of grain, but Ashentrool was described as '*bot ane gras roume for the maist part*' (i.e., most of it was only grazing). Some 50 years later, however, Ashentrool was fully settled.[31]

The locations chosen for the new farmsteads may have been influenced by the earlier pattern of shieling in the glen. From the archaeological survey there is a notable coincidence of shieling-huts with temporary intakes of arable ground on the hills, and it is likely that the concentration of stock in these areas improved the fertility of the land sufficiently to attract more permanent settlement (pp.30-1). The documentation of shieling, or transhumant grazing, is poor in the Ochils, generally occurring only in the form of passing references in evidence given during boundary disputes. True transhumant grazing may have largely died out during the 16th century. However, in 1698 shielings are mentioned in evidence before the Court of Session of a dispute between Holburn of Menstrie and Stirling of Keir, referring to events in the 1630s or even earlier.[32] One of the witnesses, John Robb in Caverkae (Alva), said that William Alexander, Earl of Stirling, pastured about 280 sheep over the summer months on the east side of the glen, moving between Greenforet by day and the hill of Menstrie by night. He had heard that about 60 years ago Menstrie's herd '*built a shield upon the ground of Greenforrest* (Greenforet) *but did never see it standing*'. In effect, by the late 17th century, the existence of earlier shielings was seen as a mechanism of affirming the ownership of tracts of hill land on the boundaries of properties, even though none of the witnesses suggested that they had been occupied as such for many years, either there or elsewhere in the Ochils. By the 1630s shieling does not appear to have been a regular element of land-use, although the term evidently continued in use into the 18th century. A tack of 1742 for Lipney refers to the '*said lands and equal halfe of the Hill pasturage and Holding houses, Biggands, yairds, Tofts, Crofts, Grasings, Shealing and all other pertinents*'.[33] By this date the reference to shielings is likely to be as much historical as relating to any practical management of grazing.

The area of arable land continued to expand through the first half of the 18th century and this is reflected in the documentation. At Lipney in 1760 it was said that '*a great deal*' of arable had been '*taken in*' since 1701, at which time there were 52 acres. A tack of 1740 to James McFarlane allowed him to take in an acre of extra arable, which he could plough only for three consecutive years; thereafter it was to be left in grass for three years before being ploughed again.[34] James Wright's notes also refer to ground being newly taken into arable in the 1750s. One aspect of this process was the episodic cultivation of what was otherwise pasture. This is probably reflected in the small patches of ephemeral, undeveloped rig recorded in the archaeological survey across the higher ground in the glen, outwith the areas enclosed by the head-dykes (e.g. fig.14).

Pre-improvement farming practice

Testaments show that oats and bear barley were the main crops, generally in a ratio of around 4:1 or 5:1; infield or croft oats gave a higher return than outfield, but outfield oats was the biggest single crop. Legumes and flax are mentioned in testaments, and, along with hemp, were grown by Wright in the 1750s. Grain crops (and legumes) also produced straw, which was used for winter feed. Wright's records from the 1750s reveal other produce: hay was cut in 'meadows'; rushes were cut for thatch; and ferns (probably bracken) were cut for animal bedding.[35]

The organisation of cropping could be highly complex, as Wright's records of sowing and reaping at Loss between 1753 and 1758 show (fig.15).[36] Each rig (and of occasion, part of a rig) could be treated as a separate unit, sown with a different crop. In 1754 the Calfward, for instance, was sown with oats.

The year after most was sown with barley, but a ridge on the north side was given over to potatoes. In 1756, oats was sown again, but, in 1757, whilst most was oats, there were also some peas. The latter did not grow, so, on 10th June, barley was sown '*where the peas was*'. In 1758, oats was sown '*in the Calfward and the tathed brae above and the piece now taken in on the west side of* (it) *up to the old Pomfold*'. The Easter Croft was treated equally flexibly, but here there is evidence of further complexity, the oat seed for neighbouring blocks of rigs being drawn from different sources. In 1753, the easterly ridges yielded some barley, but the six ridges on the west side were under oats from one source, and the rest oats from another. In 1754, part of a ridge was planted with potatoes, and the rest with oats, but there were four other groups of rigs under oats, each sown with different seed on different dates. In 1755, barley was sown where the potatoes had been, bear in the six ridges on the west side and the four on the east, and a tiny quantity of rye somewhere close by.

The management of the arable land also involved a division of crops between infield and outfield. Plots mentioned in the manuscripts, however, are rarely distinguished as infield or outfield, one rare exception being the outfield oats sown in 1756 on ground due north of Loss and east of the sheep-house (fig.15). The higher and more exposed ground above Loss was probably regarded as outfield. It was generally under oats, but, in 1755, some barley was sown there. In contrast, How Croft, which was good ground close to the steading of Loss, was probably infield. It comprised perhaps fourteen or sixteen ridges and some '*furr to furr*' ridges (the latter possibly old broad ridges that had yet to be split). Peas and beans were sown in the western furrs in 1754, at which time '*the rest of the said furrs, being old rested ley*' were under oats, and there was also part of a ridge of potatoes and ten other ridges of oats. In 1756 the How Croft was almost entirely under barley.

Ground to be sown with barley was well prepared not only with manure but also with lime. At Over Milnfold, for instance, of the nine ridges sown in 1754, three in the middle of the plot had been well limed. The application of manure was also managed carefully, both through folding stock on to the arable (see below) and by composting the bedding from byres and sheep-houses. Old thatch from buildings, some of it presumably impregnated with soot from open hearths, was also a valuable source of manure. When Backside of Lipney was repaired in 1752, James Wright recovered the '*tirrings for dung to Land to the value of nine pound Scots*', amounting to just over 10% of the bill for extensive rebuilding and repairs (p.35).[37]

It is evident from these examples that the management of arable during the 18th century, if not earlier, could be highly complex, although no overall pattern of crop rotation can be discerned from the available documentation; all that can be said in this respect is that successive crops of barley on the same ground were avoided. It is equally clear, however, that the system did not fit within a simple infield-outfield model, in which a discrete area of infield was under permanent cultivation, receiving the majority of the manure. There was a tendency for oats to be sown on higher ground, and for the transitory cultivation of pastures, most of which were presumably on hill ground, but these patterns did not necessarily manifest themselves in a discrete geographical pattern. While still a traditional farming system, during the first half of the 18th century it began also to incorporate improving techniques in land management. As early as 1722, for example, the tenant of Whittetsbank had the privilege of quarrying limestone on the Sheriffmuir for use on his land.[38] Equally, in 1746, two tenancies at Fossachie were amalgamated and it was stipulated that the tenant was not to over lime.[39]

The management of grazing and stock was intertwined with that of arable and could be equally complex. Beasts commonly grazed between fields, on stubble, on broken ground, and on the open hill. The names of several of the areas of arable,

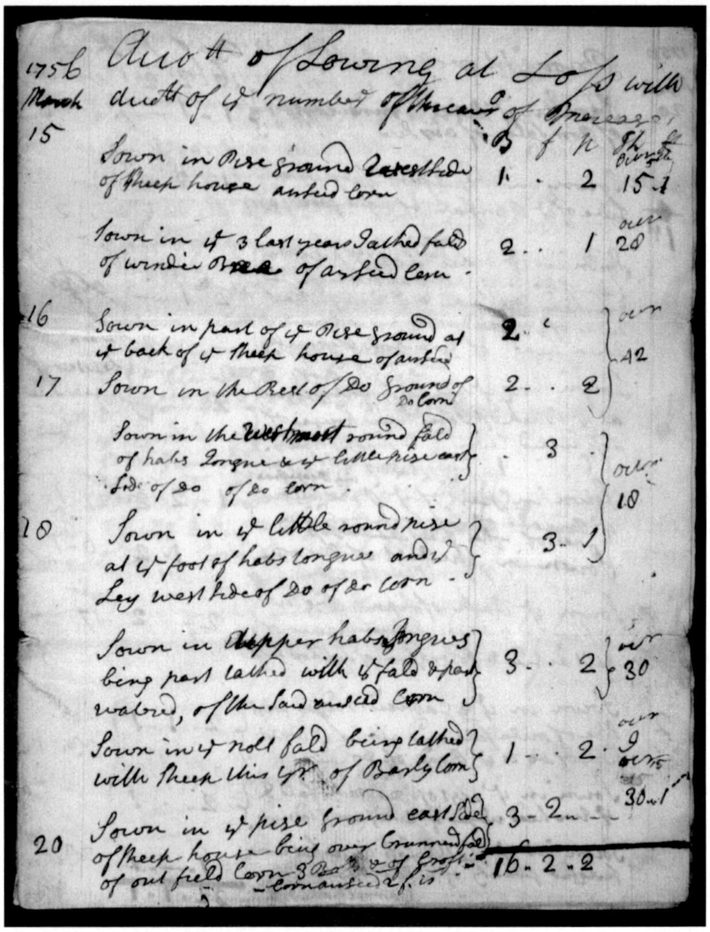

Fig.15 The complexity of the cropping arrangements that were in operation in the glen before the Improvements are illustrated by James Wright's account of sowing at Loss, March 1756, which highlights the importance of tathing in the management of arable ground. The first three columns detail the quantity of grain sown in B(ols), f(irlots) and p(ecks). The harvest, during October, is expressed in Th(reaves) and st(ouks). Wright uses Do to mean Ditto. Reproduced by permission of the Keeper of the Records of Scotland (NAS, RH/15/115/5/1, Bundle I).

1756	accott of sowing at Loss with					
march	accott of ye number of threaves of increases					
		B	f	p	Th	st
					Octr	
15	sown in Pice (piece) ground Westside of sheep house aitseed (seed oats) corn	1	.	2	15 .. 1	
					Octr	
	sown in ye 3 last years tathed falds of windie Brae of aitseed corn	1	.		28	
16	Sown in part of ye Pice ground at ye back of ye sheep house of aitseed	2	..			
					Octr	
					42	
17	Sown in the Rest of Do ground of Do corn	2	.	2		
	Sown in the westmost round fald of habs Tongue & ye little pice east side of Do of Do corn	.	3	.		
					Octr	
					18	
18	Sown in ye little round rise at ye foot of habs tongue and ye ley west side of Do of Do corn		3 .. 1			
	Sown in upper habs Tongue being part tathed with ye fald & part watered, of the said aitseed corn	3	..	2	Octr 30	
	Sown in ye nolt fald being tathed with sheep this yr of Barley corn	1	...	2	Octr 9	
					Octr 15	
20	Sown in ye pice ground eastside of sheep house being over Crunnen fold	3 .. 2 ..			30 .. 1	
	of outfield corn 3 bols & of croft corn aitseed 2 f is	16 .. 2 .. 2				

Fig.16 This oblique aerial view looks west over the pattern of banks, partial enclosures and interdigitating blocks of rigs to the north and north-west of Ashentrool. The character of the remains, with complex sequences of cultivation and enclosure, probably results from tathing, a practice in which areas of arable were manured by stock held in temporary folds. SC 611363 611363

such as Calfward and Nolt Fauld, also imply their origin as enclosures for stock. Numbers of animals were regulated, either formally or informally, to protect shared grazing rights, and stipulations to this effect were commonplace in tacks. In 1729, the tenant of Backside of Lipney for instance, was allowed to graze seven milk cows with their calves on the infield, and twelve young cattle, six horses and sixty sheep on the Common Hill, where the landlord had additional grazing rights for sheep and cattle in winter.[40] In general, management of grazing appears to have been successful, but in some cases it may have broken down. One such instance is indicated by a series of nineteen-year tacks granted in 1743 by the Keir estate, which took the extreme step of forbidding all their tenants in the area to graze any sheep at all.[41]

Other measures were also taken to protect pasture, often by laying down very specifically the areas of permitted grazing, and in some cases specifying the route by which beasts were to be herded. A good example can be seen in the tack of 1701 to the two tenants of Tounhead of Loss, James Burn in Quarterside of Lipney and Archibald Row in Tounhead, who were to share grazing including all of '*the grass from the alder tree at the head of the Little Loss on the east side to the March of Ashentrule on the west side, comprehending the Peat Gait and the West Craigs, the grass of the West Craigs to be mean* (shared or common) *grass for the use of the said Alexander* (Wright of Loss) *and them and the piece of ground called the Banks*'. Each was entitled to graze two horses, two cows, two calves (stirks) and twelve sheep. The lease was continued to Archibald Row alone on similar terms in 1704 and 1715, the latter tack stipulating grazing '*within the dykes and no further*'.[42] The dykes mentioned in the tack presumably refer to head-dykes, above which other tenants would have had grazing rights.

Wright thought that a convenient system for '*herding the hill*' was important.[43] In this respect, he evidently followed his father, who, in the tack for Tounhead in 1744, had stipulated

the route the cattle were to take to and from the hill; they were to go up the Western Loan of Loss to the Balloch in the forenoon and down by the Mine Holes in the evening.[44] Such minute control of grazing required the near-constant attendance of a herd, and Wright is known to have employed a herd in the 1750s.[45] The wages of herds are also mentioned in some testaments dating from the 17th century.

Stock brought back from the hill at night were often folded on areas that were intended to be cultivated the following season, a process called tathing. The numerous turf-walled enclosures recorded by the archaeological survey in the glen, many of them in fragmentary condition as a result of cultivation, are likely to be a product of this practice. Tathing was a standard element in many farming systems and was one of the mechanisms by which the arable was manured. The benefits of this approach must have been recognised from an early date, and it was explicitly exploited by Wright. In 1756, for example, barley was sown in the Nolt Fauld '*being tathed with sheep this year*'.[46] Sporadic cultivation of pasture would also have exploited the improved fertility of the land in areas into which grazing had concentrated, serving to maintain and enhance natural variations in soil fertility and the lushness of the sward (pp.30-1).

Animals were also penned or housed in various other ways. Sheep, for example, were sometimes accommodated in low-roofed sheep-houses (p.59). These are not only mentioned in the manuscript sources for the glen, but two examples have been identified during the course of the archaeological survey. Some of the pens, too, had specific functions. One, at Cauldhame, was a poinfold, a fold for stray animals found on the common grazing.[47] Other small enclosures, generally not more than about 20m across, which were found scattered across the glen in the course of the archaeological survey, were presumably routine gathering points for activities such as shearing. The majority of these lie on hill ground beyond the head-dykes.

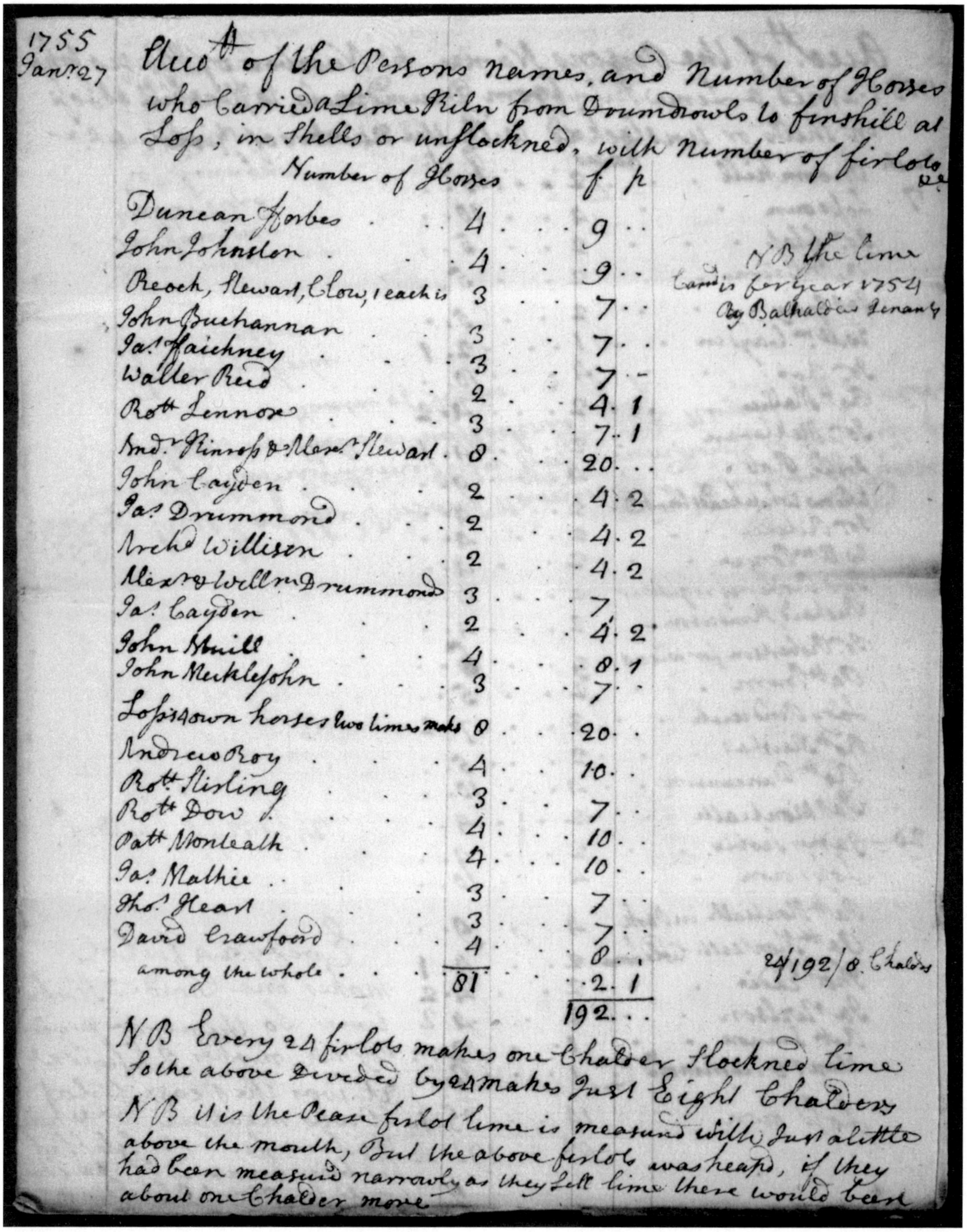

1755
Janry 27

Acco^t of the Persons names, and Number of Horses who Carried a Lime Kiln from Drumdrowls to finshill at Loss, in Shells or unslockned, with Number of firlots &c

Number of Horses		f	p
Duncan Forbes	4	9	..
John Johnston	4	9	..
Reoch, Stewart, Clow, 1 each is	3	7	..
John Buchannan	3	7	..
Jas Faichney	3	7	..
		7	-
Walter Reid	2	4	1
Robt Lennox	3	7	1
Andw Kinross & Alexr Stewart	8	20	..
John Cayden	2	4	2
Jas Drummond	2	4	2
Archd Willison	2	4	2
Alexr & Willm Drummond	3	7	
Jas Cayden	2	4	2
John Hnill	4	8	1
John Meiklejohn	3	7	.
Loss's own horses two times makes	8	20	.
Andrew Roy	4	10	..
Robt Stirling	3	7	..
Robt Dow	4	10	..
Patt Monteath	4	10	..
Jas Mathie	3	7	..
Thos Heart	3	7	..
David Crawfoord	4	8	.
among the whole	81	2	1
		192	..

N B the lime carried is for year 1754 by Balhaldies Tenants

24/192/8 Chalders

N B Every 24 firlots makes one Chalder Slockned lime So the above Divided by 24 makes Just Eight Chalders

N B it is the Pease firlot lime is measured with Just a little above the mouth, But the above firlots was heaped, if they had been measured narrowly as they sell lime there would been about one Chalder more

Fig.17 Improvements carried out by James Wright before his reorganisation of the estate of Loss included large-scale liming, reflected in his account of the carriage of lime from the nearby farm of Drumdruills, on January 27th 1755. Reproduced by permission of the Keeper of the Records of Scotland (NAS, RH15/115/5/2, Bundle F).

Menstrie Glen on the eve of improvement

By 1750 Wright was playing an active role in the management of his estates and he embarked upon a series of improvements to Loss. He renovated the house from 1751 onward (below), occupying it regularly from 1753 until at least 1763, and he also planted large numbers of trees on the estate (below and p.59). At first, however, Wright does not appear to have intended any radical reform, and his investment in the existing structure of the estate extended to at least some of the tenanted holdings: Backside of Lipney was extensively repaired in 1753 and, as late as 1757, the houses at Tounhead were thoroughly repaired, apparently using locally-grown timber.

Wright's management of stock in the 1750s was not unusual either, reflecting a traditional balance between sheep and cattle. His notes throughout the period refer to cattle, and in 1759 he sold some 20 cattle, 43 sheep, two horses and at least 15 pigs at Loss; some of these were sold on behalf of other people, but many of the others were home-reared.[48] In April 1760 he complained angrily that 20 stots, bought the previous autumn, though carefully looked after all winter and fed hay in '*straight*' weather, were still only worth what he had paid for them.[49] Comparable numbers of sheep were maintained through the 1750s, but cattle remained a mainstay throughout this period.[50]

Wright's intention of improvement rather than radical reform in the period 1753-6 can also be detected in his management of arable ground. An area called The Risk was sown with oats in 1754 having been '*drained with rumeling sivers*', and drainage was extended later to other areas.[51] Large-scale liming was also effected; for example, between January and March 1755 lime was carried from Drumdruills, to the west of the glen (figs 12 and 17), to be applied on Finshill, Loss.[52] Lesser quantities were brought in subsequent years. Wright experimented with methods of preparing the ground for planting, and in 1755 and 1756, at Little Loss, an area of '*about 5 bolls sowing of ground*' was ploughed over twelve days, obliterating the old '*furrs*' before it was harrowed and limed.[53] He also experimented with different crops. In 1753 potatoes had been grown mainly for domestic use (although he sold and gave away some seed potatoes), but from 1754 increasing quantities were planted by Wright and at least one of his tenants. Crops seen for the first time include the 18 lbs of red clover, a bushel of rye grass and some timothy grass he sowed in 1754. Thereafter, rye grass and a range of clovers feature regularly, both together and separately.[54]

The indications that more fundamental changes were in the offing come in the second half of the 1750s. The old arable was increasingly sown to pasture, whilst the poorer ground, such as that around the sheep-house and the Crunen (Crunie) Fauld on the slopes above Loss, was abandoned after 1756. The reduction in the extent of arable is reflected in the quantity of oats and barley that were being grown at Loss. In 1755, about 47 bolls were sown, but by 1758 this figure had reduced to only about 22 bolls. The importance of new crops, such as potatoes, increased also. By this time Wright appears to have been planning a radical transformation that would see the establishment of a large sheep-farming operation. His purchase of '*two fine tups for my ewes at Loss*' in 1758 suggests a conscious attempt to improve the flock in preparation for the ensuing changes.[55] He may also have been granting only short leases at this time to facilitate the removal of his tenants. The last lease for Tounhead, for example, in 1757, was for only four years. At the same time Wright began to empark the ground around his house and steading at Loss, building new stone walls and banks (see below). The creation of these policies was one of Wright's most enduring impacts on the glen.

The Loss policies

The creation of a discrete area of parkland around Loss was a considerable enhancement of the landscape, the legacy of which is the mature trees that survive today. Wright's sentiments towards trees are clear from a draft letter of 1753: '*The timber planted in the tenants yards is doing pretty well, only some few trees gone back which I intend to supply with others. The wood is growing very well I cause advertise yearly at the Church door discharging of persons from cutting it and offering a reward to anybody that will discover them. I take all the care of it I can for I think timber is both beautyful & profitable*'.[56]

The park that he created around Loss takes in the hillside to the north of the Loss Burn, and also some of the ground to the south. The dykes that enclose it are very distinctive, comprising a stone outer face embanked internally with turf, and they were probably supplemented by hedging planted on the crest of the bank (fig.18). Some of these hedges survive as landscape features nearly 250 years later. The drive to Loss approached from the south down a lime tree avenue, which survives in a fragmentary form on the south side of the Loss Burn, arcing around to approach the house from the west. This

Fig.18 This ground view looks north-westwards across the area that James Wright enclosed within his park. Loss is at the centre of the picture, immediately to the right of two isolated trees, and the main boundaries created in 1758 and 1762 can be identified from the lines of trees on the face of the hill beyond. Most of the trees that are visible were planted by Wright during the 1750s and 1760s. SC 578622

presents a magnificent view south-eastwards down the glen.

The ground work for the park was begun in the second half of the 1750s. The construction of the stockproof dykes is well recorded in Wright's papers, despite some slight discrepancies in measurements. The park boundary, defining the crescentic shape around the north of Loss, was commissioned by Wright on the 4th July 1758. Some 430m in length and laid out by stakes, it was completed by three men within 30 days (p.56, fig.51).[57] Subsequently, a second boundary was added, probably in 1762, running from Tounhead to the Mill Fauld.[58] The emparkment, however, was just one element in the enclosure of Loss, and a number of other boundaries had already been constructed in the vicinity. In 1757 three coped stone dykes were built around Loss, each 4 or 4½ feet (1.2m - 1.35m) in height.[59] These accounts can be identified with two dykes dropping down from Loss to the Loss Burn, and another from the garden to the Crunie Burn (p.49, fig.43).

Within the area Wright had emparked, large numbers of trees were planted, of which only a remnant survive, including the stands of oaks along the watercourses and the trees around Loss. Numerous other stands of trees and shelter belts were planted across his holdings on the west side of the glen, extending well beyond the ash trees of his tenants' yards, but few of these can now be identified.

An improved landscape 1760-9

From 1760 Wright effected a radical reorganisation of the landscape in the glen. New land divisions were created with the building of march-dykes and enclosures, and several sheep walks were established. He took over Lipney from his tenants, and from late 1761, he rented Fossachie from Haldane of Airthrey, while by 1762, he had successfully negotiated a new division of Lossintrule with his neighbour, Stirling of Keir.[60] Large areas of cultivated ground were turned over to pasture, often through under-sowing the last arable crop. This was the case at Fossachie, and is recorded in a note dated 31st December 1761, in which the tenants wrote: '*Sir, we agrie to your sowing grass seeds in our croft land the ensuing spring – you always satisfying us for any damage that may occasion our victual*'.[61] Shortly afterwards the tenants of Backadykes and Cadger Knowes were turned off, their houses to be knocked down unless required for incoming shepherds. Wright's memoranda show that he intended to take the same course with the lands that fell to him following the division of Lossintrule. The lease of Tounhead was probably allowed to lapse in 1761, though miners engaged on the Loss mine in 1762 may have used the houses. The eastern half of the glen followed a similar pattern; in 1760, Robert Hoge, a tenant of the hill and low ground of Myreton was being pressurised to quit by his landlord, who wanted to turn the ground to sheep.[62]

Between what he owned and rented, Wright now controlled the greater part of the glen and his main interests were in sheep. His properties were delimited by stone dykes or, in the case of a new boundary between Ashentrool and Cadger Knowes, by a bank and hedge. Internal divisions were constructed at Fossachie, but, in contrast to those at Loss,

Fig.19   *The stone dyke in the foreground of this ground view looking south-east down Menstrie Glen from near Ashentrool is one of a the new land divisions laid out in the 1760s. This example marks the march between Ashentrool and Loss, and the line of trees leading away on the left of the picture follows the boundary of the emparkment established between Loss and Tounhead. SC 584585*

these were mainly fences (palings), which were quicker and cheaper to construct than stone walls. While these changes could take place very quickly, the transformation of the ground to a sheep walk needed time, in particular in allowing the new pasture to establish itself. In this respect Wright was prepared to be patient. In March 1763, a Mr McAdam wrote to him offering to supply 120 big ewes, suggesting that they would be well suited to his purpose of stocking the land with breeding ewes.[63] However, Wright replied that '*this being the first year of Fossachie and the grass not in very good order, I'm afraid it would* (have) *been too soon*'. Nevertheless, Wright promised to accept 60 to 80 lambs as soon as they were fit to travel.

Numbers of sheep rose steeply and, by late 1763, there were around 370 on Fossachie. Shortly after, in 1767, there were about 500 sheep on Fossachie and Lipney; most of them were breeding ewes, but there were also 90 'highland' wedders, presumably lambs bought in for fattening. Selective breeding initiated as early as 1758 (above),[64] was continuing in 1763 using six English tups.[65] The system of land-management had changed too, with a prevalence of sown grass, an increase in hay production, the use of turnips for forage (below), and the careful organisation of enclosures to optimise the grazing.[66]

Goats were also being kept on the farms of Lipney and Fossachie. Their milk was a fashionable health drink, which spawned a small specialised tourist industry centred on Blairlogie. This had '*long been a favourite resort for invalids*', one of the attractions being the availability of goats' whey.[67]

A draft advertisement for Lipney in 1760 says that '*the tenant may keep goats in a den very fit for the purpose where they used to be keept and there is a great demand for the milk being so near a populos Country*' (pp.12-13, fig.5). An appended note suggests that 40 goats were kept there in 1701.[68] Wright's notes show that after 1761 he kept some 35 to 40 goats at Fossachie, and 34 goats were sold to Adam Bennet in Blairlogie at the final sale of Wright's goods after his death.[69] The fashion for goats' whey seems to have faded during the middle years of the 19th century, by which time the spa at Bridge of Allan had become an invincible rival to Blairlogie.

Wright now managed his holdings in Menstrie Glen as part of a much larger, integrated operation with rented ground elsewhere. In 1763 he wrote to Mr Haldane in Doune to inform him that he could not '*follow my plan to the heights I intended by feeding them on turneeps after coming from the mountains without getting your Airthrey low parks*'.[70] The fields were duly rented, as was land at Craigton, Leckie, and Bridgehaugh to the west of Stirling, at Frandy in Glen Devon, and at Alva, east of Menstrie. These holdings allowed a much more flexible approach to managing his stock than if he had been limited to the Menstrie holdings alone, and there is evidence that Wright was moving the stock freely between them. Where necessary, beasts could be moved to winter grass or hay, lean stock could be sent to rich pasture to fatten for market, and breeding ewes could be fed up to improve their condition prior to lambing.[71]

Fig.20   This ground view looks south-east down Menstrie Glen from the southern flank of Loss Hill. The landscape is virtually empty now, populated only by sheep, the ultimate conclusion of the rationalisation of the holdings and the changes in land management set in train by James Wright in the 1760s. SC 579491

Although sheep were now clearly Wright's main interest, his droving business was now strongly developed and involved several hundred beasts every year, mainly moving direct from the Highlands to markets in the Lowlands. A small annual cattle sale at Loss, usually held in November, was an extension of this business.[72] Some of the cattle in the sale had been bought in to be fattened, but others had been reared in the glen. In November 1767 there were up to sixty cattle at Fossachie.[73] Furthermore, Wright did not abandon arable in Menstrie Glen altogether, although it was clearly much less important than it had been hitherto. There are references to sowing and reaping, reflecting a low-level arable component in the land-use of the glen that continued until at least the end of the 19th century. Pollen analysis, however, suggests that by about 1800 cereals were no longer being grown on the higher ground, such as the hill above Ashentrool.[74]

James Wright died in late 1769, by which time the greater part of the Ochils appears to have been turned over to sheep. He may have been bankrupt at the time and his holdings were broken-up. The sale of the farm stock of Fossachie, Frandy and Aithrey illustrates the emphasis on sheep; the 1015 sheep at Frandy were all bought by John Robb, the tenant of Jerah, a clear indication that Wright's nearest neighbour in the glen was also concentrating on sheep. A further 400 sheep and around 40 cattle were probably at Fossachie.[75] Loss and Lipney were inherited by his cousin, the minister of Logie, also called James Wright, who rented them to James Drummond of Balnacoul, before selling up to John Gray by 1778.[76]

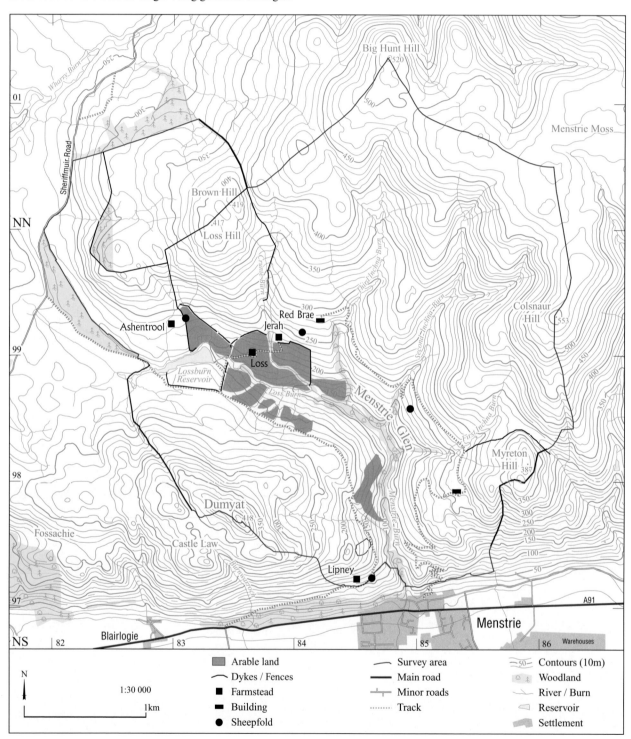

Fig.21 This map depicts the extent of arable ground and settlement in the early 19th century, and reveals the dramatic contraction of settlement that took place after the reorganisation of the landscape in the 1760s (compare with fig.11).

The late 18th century and after

The documentation of activity in Menstrie Glen effectively died with Wright, and relatively little is known thereafter. In 1782 John Robb, the tenant of Jerah, rented Loss for two years. In an echo of the arrangement between Wright and his tenants at Lipney twenty years earlier, Robb was to allow the landlord to undersow his arable with grass in the second year.[77] Arable cultivation in the glen evidently continued, but it was a diminishing component in the economy. By 1803 the tenant of Loss had to observe a strict rotation of crops and grass, and apply at least 20 bolls of lime yearly to the arable. Most of the arable was to be under green crops, such as potatoes or turnips, and grass was to be sown at the rate of 12 lb clover and 5 lb rye grass per acre.[78] During the course of the 19th century arable appears to have been concentrated in the lower reaches of the glen around Loss, Lipney and Jerah.

The trend towards increasingly large holdings, set in train by Wright in the 1760s, continued into the 19th century. In 1813, John Robb's son, Alexander, who had succeeded him as the tenant of Jerah, offered to rent Loss and Lipney jointly for nineteen years, placing the greater part of the glen under Robb's control.[79] An undated plan of Loss and Lipney,[80] which may date to this period, shows patches of arable along the west bank of the Menstrie Burn from Foreside of Lipney to Backside of Lipney (not depicted) and around Loss. The arable, however, only adds up to a little over 10% of the total acreage, and the rest is shown set to pasture. As part of the agreement with Alexander Robb, the landlord was to build a new house at Lipney, and Robb was given an allowance on his rent on account of defective fences. Other tenancies had also been amalgamated by this time. Ploverburn, Ashentrool, Longcraig, Whittetsbank and Callendar were amalgamated in stages from the late 18th century to about 1810.[81] The tenancy of Whittetsbank was terminated in 1763, while Longcraig survived until 1793; Ploverburn, where the tenant agreed to quit at Whitsunday 1762,[82] was formally merged with Ashentrool between 1811 and 1813. On the neighbouring estate, Abercromby of Aithrey renewed Andrew Roy's lease of Fossachie, Cadger Knowes and Broomhill for nineteen years from 1807, and added Back a Dykes, which had until recently been leased to John Neilson.[83] Here too, a minor arable component is reflected in the lease, which stipulated that the old crofting ground of Fossachie and Back a Dykes was to be kept in half barley, half oats, alternately until the final three years, when all was to be kept as grass.

The process of withdrawal from the old farmsteads and the transfer of arable land into pasture continued into the mid-19th century. Ashentrool had been abandoned by 1841,[84] and Loss, which was occupied by farm servants in 1841,[85] was derelict by 1851.[86] By now most of the glen was set to pasture,[87] although a ploughman and a dairymaid were employed at Jerah as late as 1861. By that stage Jerah and Lipney were the only occupied sites in the glen.[88]

Ironically, knowledge of the most recent management of the glen in the late 19th and 20th century is poor, but sheep continued to dominate here, as elsewhere in the Ochils.[89] The only subsequent major changes of land-use in the glen saw the construction of the Lossburn reservoir after Water Orders were issued in 1897 and 1915,[90] and the establishment of small coniferous plantations within and at the edges of the survey area in the 1940s and 1950s.

Fig.22 The shattered shell of the 19th century farmhouse at Jerah, seen from the north and looking to Dumyat beyond. SC 585584

THE SETTLEMENTS

The expansion of settlement in Menstrie Glen reached its zenith about 1700. With the depopulation of the glen from 1760 onwards, most of the farmsteads were soon abandoned, and their remains have lain undisturbed ever since. These farmsteads have been recorded in the course of the archaeological survey, but there is also a wider range of settlement evidence surviving in the glen, ranging from the huts and bothies of summer shielings to the cottages of the 19th-century shepherds. The settlement remains that have been identified can be grouped under five headings, each reflecting the character of the structural evidence. Firstly, and probably the earliest in date, there are the shielings, each comprising a cluster of stone and turf huts. Secondly, there is a scatter of large turf buildings and byre-houses, the latter almost certainly small farmsteads. Thirdly, there is a series of stone-built farmsteads, their buildings and enclosures arranged in a more-or-less regular plan (see p.37, fig.31 for comparative plans). Fourthly, there is the relatively grand house and steading at Loss. Finally, there are the shells of several 19th-century buildings. At Foreside of Lipney, the only farm to remain in use and now known as Dumyat, the farm buildings were replaced in the 20th century and are still occupied.

With the exception of the settlements consisting of large turf buildings, the morphological differences between the various categories of settlement are relatively clear cut. The 18th-century stone-built farmsteads are of a type familiar throughout the uplands of eastern Scotland, while the late 19th- and 20th-century cottages and steadings are readily identifiable by their mortared walls or, where they have been destroyed, from the map sources. The main shieling groups also present few problems of identification. The large turf buildings, however, pose more general problems of classification and interpretation. Several of them have been found in isolated locations, while others lie within shieling groups, though it is not always clear whether they date from the original use of the shielings or represent a later reuse of those sites. The form of these buildings rarely gives any clue to their function, their possible uses ranging from dwellings to sheep-houses. In seven cases, however, including two that lie within shieling groups, the morphological characteristics of the buildings have allowed them to be identified as byre-houses (see below), and these in turn have been interpreted as farmsteads with some confidence. Indeed, one of them, superimposed on a shieling at Cadger Knowes, can probably be identified from the documentary sources with a small-holding occupied in the mid-18th century (p.32).

The shieling groups are potentially the earliest of the settlement remains, representing a pattern of seasonal land-use that has its origins at least as early as the medieval period. Nothing is visible of any permanent settlements of equivalent date, but both Jerah and Lipney may have originated as medieval farms, and there is likely to have been a third, undocumented, medieval settlement on the east side of the valley, perhaps at Inchney. The main weight of the archaeological remains, however, including the turf farmsteads, is almost certainly post-medieval in date, a manifestation of the intense activity recorded in the 17th- and 18th-century documentation. This intensity accounts for the complex patterns of rig and enclosures on all the spurs, which has severely limited the chances of any earlier settlements surviving on the lower slopes. It can also be seen in the fact that at least twelve of the fourteen stone-built farmsteads visible today were occupied in the 18th century, and the other two are also almost certainly of this date.

Shielings

The practice of shieling or transhumant grazing is poorly documented in the Ochils (p.21). Nevertheless, clusters of shieling-huts are amongst the commonest types of settlement evidence recorded by the archaeological survey. Sixteen groups have been identified, mainly occurring on the ground above 300m OD. Typically they lie close to a burn, in a sheltered spot on, or at least close to, good quality grazing. Each cluster may comprise up to twelve separate structures, most of which are small turf-built huts, but a number of larger buildings may also be included, some of which have stone footings. The huts generally measure 2m to 3m internally, but also extend to 6.3m by 3.5m internally, while the buildings may be considerably larger, measuring up to 13m in internal length.

The shielings on the northern flank of Dumyat provide good examples of the variety of structures that occur on these sites. Two of the clusters of huts and buildings are situated about 100m apart on Cadger Knowes. The upper cluster lies on a grassy terrace, its huts broadly representative of those elsewhere in the glen. Amongst them, however, there is a larger building, in this case measuring 8.9m by 3.3m internally, attached to which is a small enclosure. The lower cluster comprises a single hut and four buildings, the westernmost of which is a large byre-house, described below (p.32). The remaining buildings are also of considerable size, measuring about 13m in length internally, and it is not clear whether these should be considered as part of the shieling, or perhaps more permanent habitations, and some may even be sheep-houses. A similar combination of huts and buildings lies some 850m to the east, midway between Backside and Quarterside of Lipney (p.47, fig.41).

Comparable groups of structures occur on the opposite side of the glen, where there is at least one group that is unusual for the number of larger buildings it includes. This group lies beyond the head-dyke above Little Jerah (p.51, fig.45) and comprises at least nine huts and buildings. The huts here have a single compartment and measure a little over 5m in length by 3m transversely within turf walls spread up to 1.2m in thickness, but the buildings have two compartments, and measure more than 11m in length. In some of these cases, however, it is possible that the two compartments represent separate periods of occupation and construction on the same site, but there are also two single-compartment buildings of equivalent size.

What little evidence is available in the historical sources for transhumant grazing in the Ochils suggests that the practice had largely died out by the end of the 16th century, though references to shieling persist into the 18th century. The majority of these late references, however, concern boundary disputes, and the continued use of some shielings was evidently no more than a mechanism for asserting property rights. The example of Greenforet to the north of the glen, allegedly still in use in the 1630s, has already been cited (p.21), and similar disputes are documented in nearby Glen Devon.[91]

Be that as it may, the overall pattern of shielings clearly influenced the subsequent establishment of permanent settlements. The majority of the shielings lie above the head-dykes, but their distribution includes a number of groups that were subsumed into the more intensively managed ground below the dykes, albeit probably some time after the practice had been discontinued. This is what happened at Cadger Knowes, where a farmstead was established on the site of a shieling, on the fringes of an area of cultivation. A similar history of occupation is apparent at the turf-built farmstead on Loss Hill (pp.32-3, fig.26). Early in the process of settlement expansion, former shieling grounds may have proved attractive locations for new farms. Not only would grazing have improved the sward, but patterns of herding on the hill, as documented at Greenforet, would have seen the transfer of nutrients in manure from the poorer ground to the best pasture. In this way grazing stock would have improved soil fertility in discrete patches. The small-scale cultivation of common grazing along the north flank of Dumyat, for example, from

Cadger Knowes to Ston Hill above Quarterside of Lipney (p.47, fig.41), probably exploited areas improved as a result of earlier patterns of grazing. The observation of the benefits of grazing for the improvement of hill land may have contributed to the development of tathing.

Turf buildings and farmsteads
Substantial turf buildings occur at fourteen locations throughout the glen, and at seven of them the remains appear to be those of a byre-house, a type of structure in which the people were housed at one end and cattle in the other. In some cases, the byre is indicated by the shallow groove of a drain running down the centre of one half of the interior of the building; in others, its presence is indicated by a slight hollowing at one end, the hollow probably produced by repeated mucking-out of the byre. The dual function of dwelling and byre has been taken to indicate that these particular buildings were farmsteads in their own right, and at most sites there is what appears to be an associated outbuilding or an enclosure nearby. For the most part, the other large turf buildings are all isolated structures, though, as has been seen, some occur within shieling groups.

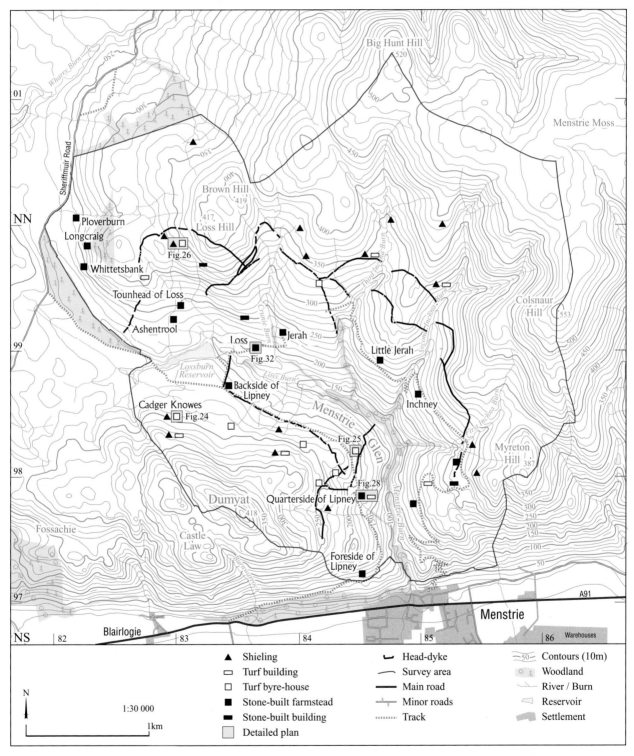

Fig.23 This map shows the dense distribution of settlements in the glen dating from before the reorganisation of the landscape in the 1760s, and is set against the pattern of head-dykes. Many of the boundaries between the main tenancies are marked by major topographical features, such as the deeply incised gullies of the burns.

31

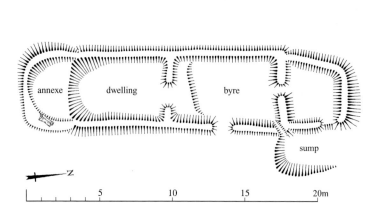

Fig.24 This plan (1:250) shows the probable mid-18th-century byre-house at Cadger Knowes, the sunken portion at the north end indicating the position of the byre, with a drain through the north-east angle into a sump or midden.

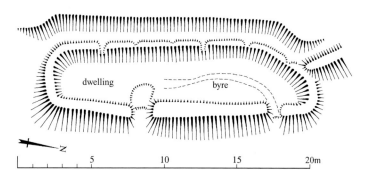

Fig.25 This plan (1:250) of the byre-house north of Quarterside of Lipney shows the position of the byre-drain in the north half of the interior, emptying through a gap in the east wall. In this case the whole of the interior is dug into the slope.

Three of the byre-houses have been surveyed in detail and they are described below to illustrate the morphological variation found amongst these structures. These are Cadger Knowes and Quarterside of Lipney, situated on the north and east flanks of Dumyat respectively, and the example on Loss Hill to the north of Ashentrool.

The turf-walled byre-house of Cadger Knowes (fig.24) is situated within a patch of rig on a gently-sloping terrace. It is the westernmost of a cluster of four buildings and a hut, elements of which probably belong to an earlier shieling. The original composition of the shieling is uncertain, however, and it is possible that the other buildings, which are of considerable size, belong to the farmstead. The byre-house measures 13.3m by 3.5m internally and lies across the contour. It has two compartments, of which the lower was the byre. The doorway was in the east wall of the byre, through which the upper, or domestic end, of the building must have been accessed. Initially, the byre seems to have been drained through a gap in the north end, but the addition of an extension at that end necessitated the diversion of the drain through a new cut in the east side to a sump outside the building. The relationship of an annexe on the south to the main building is ambiguous; while it may have been an addition to increase the internal space, it could equally be a fragment of an earlier building. The presence of a farmstead at Cadger Knowes is referred to in documentation dating to the 1750s and early 1760s,[92] which shows that it was one of the poorest holdings in the glen. It is appropriate that the farmstead should have been built of turf, but there is necessarily some doubt as to whether the documents refer to the byre-house itself or, perhaps, one of the other large buildings nearby.

The byre-house near Quarterside of Lipney, which lies above the head-dyke some 300m to the north of the well-documented, stone-walled farmstead (pp.34-5), is levelled into the back of a small terrace (fig.25). An enclosure has been added to the east side of the building, riding over the footings of a small hut to the north. The byre-house measures 16m by 3m internally, narrowing slightly at the north end, and lies along the slope, the ground rising steeply from the western wall. The northern half of the interior was the byre, with a central drain emptying out through a gap in the wall near the north-east corner. The domestic space lay in the southern half.

A drain along the back of the house diverted water from the slope above away from the interior. Six notches are visible in the crest of west wall, disposed at intervals of between 2m and 2.8m; their origin is uncertain, but it is possible that they mark the position of cruck-trusses in the base of a turf wall. This farmstead lies immediately outside the head-dyke that probably belonged to the early 18th-century farm of Quarterside, before it was amalgamated as part of the holdings of Backside and Foreside after about 1730 (p.47, fig.41).

The Quarterside byre-house is subtly different from the Cadger Knowes example. It is less regular on plan and has no visible subdivisions. This variation may reflect no more than the effect of the local topography and the use of wooden partitions, but it may point to the Quarterside building being a little earlier in date, perhaps late 17th century (but see below). A similarly irregular ground-plan is also present in the third example, which is situated amongst a group of turf-walled structures set on a terrace on the west flank of Loss Hill (figs 26, 27A). Three of the buildings are relatively small and are indistinguishable from the shieling-huts to the north-west and elsewhere in the glen. The fourth building, however, is much larger, measuring 10.2m by 3.4m internally, and the floor in the southern half of the interior is slightly sunken, suggesting that it has been a byre; the building also has an annexe added on to its north-east end.

With the exception of Cadger Knowes, the historical evidence is of little assistance in establishing the chronological or social context of these farmsteads. At face value, however, the use of turf in their construction, which has a long tradition in Scottish vernacular architecture,[93] their positions on poorer ground outside the head-dykes, and the presence of an earlier turf-walled building beneath the stone-built farmstead at Quarterside of Lipney (p.34, fig.28), can be marshalled as evidence that they are of relatively early date, representing an undocumented peak in the extent of settlement before the 18th century. Against this must be set the example at Cadger Knowes, which appears to have been occupied in the mid-18th century.

A more illuminating line of enquiry concerns the positions in which the turf-built farmsteads are found in the landscape. These contrast markedly with those of the stone-built farmsteads. The latter consistently occupy the lower slopes,

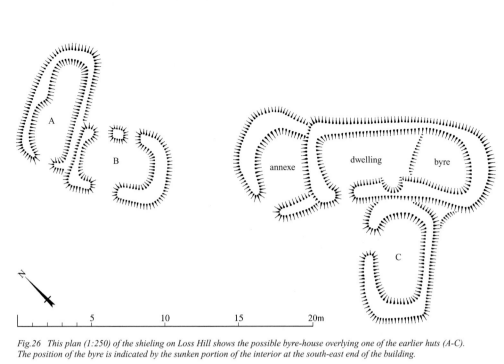

Fig.26 *This plan (1:250) of the shieling on Loss Hill shows the possible byre-house overlying one of the earlier huts (A-C). The position of the byre is indicated by the sunken portion of the interior at the south-east end of the building.*

amidst complex cultivation remains and enclosures, whereas the byre-houses, and indeed the majority of the other larger turf buildings, are situated on the fringes of the intensively cultivated ground, usually above the head-dykes. Many lie beside small patches of poorly developed rig, a particularly noticeable feature of Cadger Knowes and the other sites on the north flank of Dumyat (p.47, fig.41). None of these farmsteads is demonstrably associated with the adjacent cultivation remains, and caution is particularly necessary in the light of the allowance in some of the 18th-century tacks of the main farms for temporary intakes above the head-dyke. Nevertheless, the occupants of the turf-built farmsteads did not have access to the same quantity or quality of arable ground as those of the main farmsteads.

Rather than indicating an early date, the use of turf in the byre-houses is probably a measure of the poverty of their occupants and of the levels of investment by their landlords. In short, these were the farmsteads attached to the smaller and poorer holdings, and, like Cadger Knowes, are likely to be of 18th-century date. In practice, few of the holdings can have

generated sufficient revenue to justify any investment by the landlord. Indeed, on Loss, the documents suggest that Wright rarely troubled to improve even the buildings of the main farms, and this only when necessary (p.35). The replacement of a turf building with stone, revealed by the archaeological survey at Quarterside of Lipney, is best seen as an indication of investment in one steading, rather than as evidence of a more general chronological relationship between the use of turf and stone in construction work.

Although the other turf buildings can be conveniently grouped in the same category on morphological grounds, it is clear that they need not all share the same date or function. Some of those occurring in the shielings may well be of medieval date, but others may be the settlements of subtenants or cottars in the glen who have escaped notice in the 17th- and 18th-century documents. However, the identification of all of these buildings as dwellings is far from certain and, in some instances, they may represent sheep-houses.

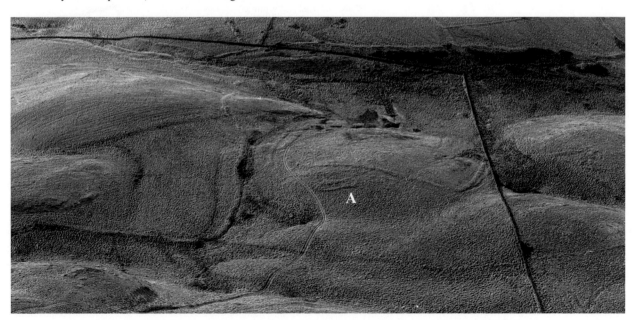

Fig.27 *The turf-walled building (A) on the west flank of Loss Hill lies beside three smaller shieling-huts, not visible on this aerial view. SC 611367*

Stone-built farmsteads

The archaeological survey has identified fourteen farmsteads built of stone (figs 23 and 31). Of these, no fewer than twelve can be identified with settlements named in 17th - and 18th-century documents, and it is reasonable to assume that the visible remains of all fourteen are of broadly similar date.

The general locations of these farmsteads have already been mentioned: they tend to be on the broad, gently-sloping terrace that separates the main watercourses from the steeper slopes running up onto the hilltops, and more particularly at the interface of the intensively cultivated arable fields on the lower slopes and the patchwork of cultivation and grazing that characterises the higher ground below the head-dyke. Their overall distribution is largely conditioned by the topography, which in many parts of the glen is broken up into natural units by deeply incised watercourses. This is a particularly prominent feature of the north and east of the glen, where the natural boundaries between the farm units are supplemented by head-dykes cutting across the intervening spurs of ground (p.31, fig.23). Even where these natural divisions are not present, for example on the north face of Dumyat, the spacing of the farms is as regular as it is on the north-east of the glen.

The character of these farmsteads is most clearly illustrated at Quarterside of Lipney, where there is a fortuitous combination of good documentary sources and a clear sequence of archaeological remains. As they survive today, the ruins of this farmstead comprise the footings of at least five buildings, one of which displays evidence of at least four distinct phases of construction (fig.28). The earliest was probably a long turf-walled building, and it was accompanied by an adjacent enclosure (A on plan). Today, the east end of this turf building can be seen protruding from beneath the later structures. In the second phase, a smaller, stone building was constructed over the west half of the turf building (B); the east end of this stone building was then dismantled and a stone byre added in its place, forming a two-compartment byre-house ranged along the north side of a yard (C). At a late stage in the occupation of the site the byre may have stood on its own (D). The perimeter of the yard incorporates fragments of an earlier stone building on the west and what may have been a free-standing barn on the south, with two garden enclosures lying to the east completing the layout. The gardens contain rich, deep soil, presumably enhanced by midden material. This would have been composted before it was spread, perhaps providing an explanation for the mound at the foot of the west wall of the northern plot.

The impression of the farmstead drawn from the survey can be fleshed-out, to some extent, from the documentary sources.

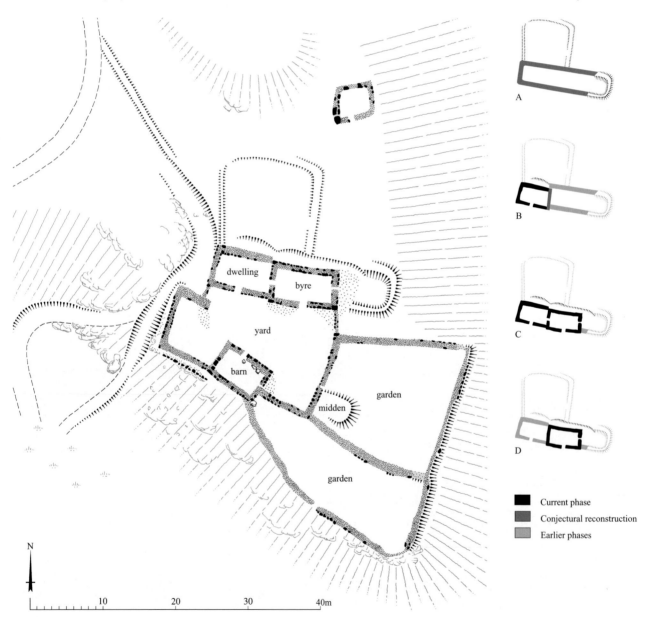

Fig.28 This plan (1:500) shows the complex remains of the stone-built 18th-century farmstead at Quarterside of Lipney. The sequence of construction of the buildings on the north side of the yard is drawn out on the right; tones have been employed to indicate the conjectural components of each phase, green represents the earlier elements at each stage of development.

These provide a limited chronological framework for its occupation, as well as illuminating aspects of the construction and function of its buildings. The establishment of the farm probably occurred with the expansion of settlement in the glen during the 16th and 17th centuries, while in the period leading up to 1730 it appears to have been a distinct holding. Thereafter Quarterside pertained either to Foreside or Backside, until it was abandoned during the late 18th century.

The form and functions of the buildings at Quarterside are illustrated in the documentation for repairs to the farmstead in 1730,[94] after John Galloway, the previous tenant, had moved out. Dated 24th February 1730, the first element of this documentation comprises a statement of what repairs were necessary and an estimate of the expense:

Ane Accompt of what expenses it will take to build and repair the houses of quarter Side off Lipnoch the house of quarter Sid consisting off Dwelling house barn and Stable and byre containing Four stone gavells & six couples being sixtie six ffoots of length in heall All to rebuild

	£ sh d
Imprimis Six couples at £3 Scots per piece, Inde	18 00 00
Item 18 trees for pan and rofffe at 10sh per pice	09 00 00
Item 14 dozen of keabers att 12s Scots per dozen Inde	08 08 00
Item two doors & door chicks & Locks Inde	03 12 00
Item for building the stone work & reading the walls and providing the morter 16 lib 10s Scots	16 10 00
Item for casting the divets winning and leading & thicking the houses 3lib Scots	03 00 00
Item for the Carriadges of the heall timber reckoned at 55 lead att 4s per lead Inde	11 00 00
	69 10 00

The second element was the eventual bill:

The houses of quarter side hes contained four stone gavells and six couples sett upon the grownd att 4lib per pice

is 24 lib	24 00 00
The roff	06 00 00
The Pantries 9 lib	09 00 00
Item 12 dozen of Keabers 12 lib	12 00 00
Item tuo doors Locks and window and bands	08 00 00
Item workmanship meat & drink Carriages and others servers 24 lib scots	24 00 00
	83 00 00

From the estimate it is possible to infer several details about the buildings of the farmstead at this time. They clearly had mortared stone walls and gables, although whether the mortar was of clay or lime is not stated, and it is reasonable to suppose these were load-bearing. This form of construction was a development of traditional construction techniques, and the crucks (i.e. '*couples sett upon the grownd*') may not have been strictly necessary to support the roof.[95] There were windows, which were presumably glazed if the bands for holding the panes are anything to go by, but the tenant may have been required to provide his own glass. Unfortunately, neither the estimate nor the bill provides a contemporary description of the layout of the farmstead, and there is no simple correlation between the documents and the visible archaeological remains. The presence of at least two buildings can be inferred from the four gables, but their overall length of 66 feet (*c.*20m) cannot be resolved with any combination of the buildings there today. One building is almost certainly represented by the range on the north side of the yard, but before the byre was built over its east end. The other may be the barn on the south, but it might equally be the fragmentary building on the west.

Estimates and bills for repairs to other farmsteads in the glen provide comparable details of their composition and

the character of their buildings. The repairs appear to have been piecemeal, probably tied to the periodic renewal of the leases, and the documentary sources paint a picture of a gradual process prompted only by necessity. Apart from the wholesale reconstruction of the house and steading at Loss in the 1750s, the farmsteads in the glen are generally the product of incremental rebuilding and repair. This seems to be the case at Backside of Lipney in 1752, where repairs were thought necessary to one of the houses, the byre, the sheep-house, the barn and a kiln, but '*the house possessed by Gray is pretty right*'.[96] This work was carried out at Wright's expense in June and July 1753, and included a total of 55½ man-days work by the cowans (rough-stone builders). Two horses transported stones and mortar for eight days, timber was cut locally and carried to the house, and divots were cast for the thatch and feal for the wall-heads. Eight new couples were supplied with '*pan*' and roof, and there are payments for '*binding 8 cuples to the sitt house and byre*'. Two large and two small windows were supplied but, in common with Quarterside, there is no mention of glass. Wright also noted that he did not supply the straw for thatch, but recovered the old thatch to be used as manure (p.21).

At first sight the farmstead appears to have been extensively rebuilt, but the precise extent of the repairs is contained in a footnote. This adds that '*The foresaid Account is for rebuilding the sitt house & byre, they were both out at the found & rebuilt & part of the gavill & one of ye side walls of the Barn was built & the half of the Barn tirred & got in a New Cuple & timber & the said House, Byre & ye part of the barn tirred was well thaked with Divots but got no Straw from me?*'.[97] This note confirms that the work was no more than remedial, for example in the rebuilding of only one side of the barn.

A similar picture emerges at Foreside of Lipney, where repairs in 1730 involved the dwelling house, two barns, a stable and byre, two sheep-houses and a corn kiln.[98] Some 30 years later, in 1760, a 'mansion house' at Foreside mentioned in a tack of 1732 was in need of repairs or rebuilding if it was to be re-let.[99] This house is likely to have dated from the early 17th century, when Lipney was '*in mainsing*'.[100]

Ongoing repairs and occasional rebuilding are also recorded at Tounhead of Loss, where there were two houses. In 1756 Robert Stirling was paid for three days '*bigging*' the yard at Tounhead, though this can only have amounted to repairs.[101] One house was repaired in 1756 and the work included binding couples and mixing mortar.[102] Further work the following year, presumably on the other house, involved '*clearing out found & tirring ditto*', which implies a certain amount of demolition.[103] Materials supplied included three couples, turves, three big window cases and two small ones, a '*stouk of thack*' and some '*myre thack*' (presumably straw and rushes). Four men spent a day putting up a lum, a division through the house and a hallan (screen). Doors and shutters were supplied.[104] Further repairs to one of the houses in 1762 involved 33 man-days work, but there are no details of what work was carried out.[105]

In several instances the estimates and accounts for repairs mention kilns, which are also a feature of the farmsteads recognised in the archaeological survey. Their distribution across the glen, however, is far from even. While kilns have been recorded in the field at Loss, Ashentrool and Backside of Lipney, and the presence of another is documented at Foreside of Lipney,[106] none have been noted outside Wright's estate on the east side of the valley from Jerah to Myreton, nor is there one at Quarterside. This distribution may simply reflect the pattern of principle farms, with kilns located at Foreside and Backside of Lipney, for instance, but not at Quarterside. That said, the absence of kilns on the east side of the valley is less easy to explain, and it is possible that it reflects some aspect of the control that the neighbouring estate exercised over its tenants. The best-preserved example in the glen has been dug into the bank of a burn at Ashentrool. The kiln-bowl measures

Fig.29 This oblique aerial photograph from the north-east provides a contrasting view to fig.40 (p.46) of the hillside around the turf byre-house (A) north of Quarterside of Lipney. The head-dyke (B), which is faintly discernible extending obliquely across the picture from top left to bottom right, is one of the later elements visible in the picture, cutting across the enclosures and rigs (C) in the immediate vicinity of the byre-house. SC 579475

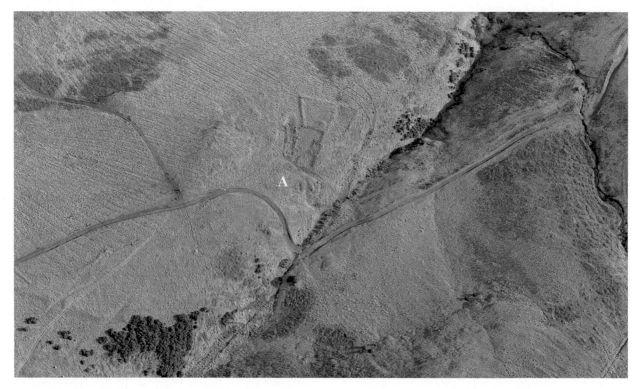

Fig.30 Nearly vertical aerial view, with east to the top, of the stone-built farmstead of Quarterside of Lipney (A), showing the disposition of buildings around the yard and the two garden enclosures to the top of the image (see also fig. 28). SC 579474

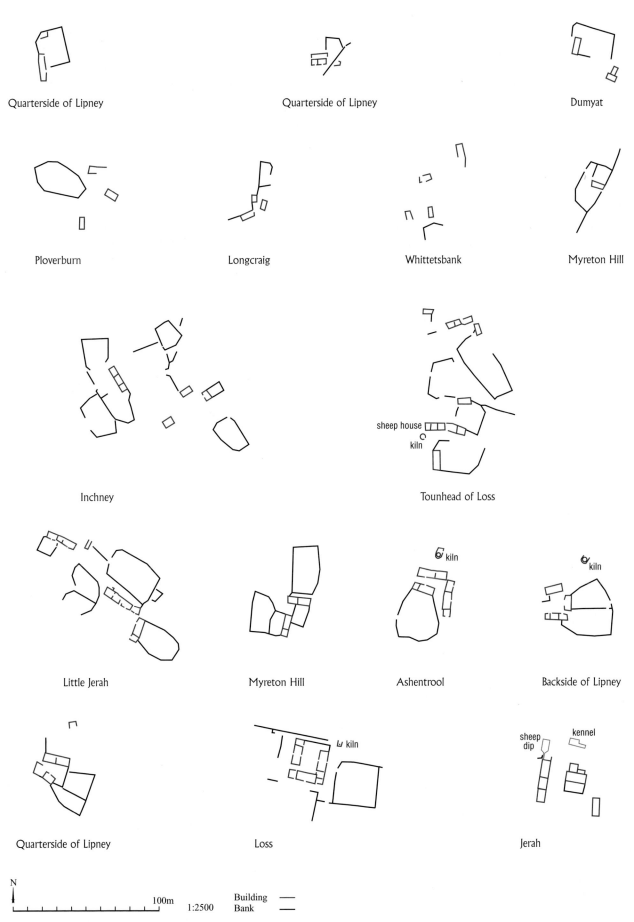

Quarterside of Lipney

Quarterside of Lipney

Dumyat

Ploverburn

Longcraig

Whittetsbank

Myreton Hill

Inchney

Tounhead of Loss

sheep house

kiln

Little Jerah

Myreton Hill

Ashentrool

kiln

Backside of Lipney

kiln

Quarterside of Lipney

Loss

kiln

Jerah

sheep dip

kennel

N

100m

1:2500

Building ———
Bank ———

Fig.31 The farmsteads within the glen dsplay a range of layouts, from the strictly formal plan of the improved steading at Loss (see also fig.32) to the more haphazard arrangement of buildings at Ploverburn or Whittetsbank. The uppermost row are turf-built, and are probably the farmsteads of the poorest tenants. However, the contrast between, for example, Ploverburn and Little Jerah suggests that a similar range of status probably exist amongst the stone-built farmstead.

2.7m in diameter and is at least 1m in depth. A slight ledge around the lip of the bowl may mark the original height of the drying-floor, and on the north side there is a barn measuring 2.6m by 1.9m internally.

To a certain extent the repairs that are recorded involve the gradual improvement of the Lipney farmsteads and the Tounhead buildings, but they in no way match the major renovations that were to take place at Loss (see below). More importantly, however, these accounts provide a general picture of the typical stone-built farmstead in the first half of the 18th century. Usually comprising at least a house, a byre and stable, and a barn, they also had a range of other features, including sheep-houses, kilns and gardens. The houses all seem to have been cruck-framed, with thatched roofs, and most probably had gables, but the only mention of a chimney is in the repairs at Tounhead in 1757. This also mentions the sub-division of the interior. Windows seem to have been a regular feature, although whether glazed or closed with shutters is not clear.

With the dramatic transformation of the glen from 1760, most of the farmsteads were abandoned. Nevertheless, the incoming shepherds needed housing, and it is conceivable that elements of the earlier farmsteads were maintained after their leases lapsed. Indeed, the stipulation that some of the tenant's houses might be required for incoming shepherds is explicitly stated in an agreement between Wright and Robert Duncanson in 1763: '*Since you* (Wright) *have been so good as allow me* (Duncanson) *to stay in the houses of Backadykes ...I hereby promise to flitt at Whitsunday next ... and if the herd come from the south before then I promise to accommodate him with a part of the house and you may tirr or throw down the rest of the houses except the sitt house when you please*'.[107] This may explain why both Backside of Lipney and Ploverburn are depicted on Stobie's map of the glen in 1783,[108] fourteen and twenty-one years respectively after they are last documented as tenanted farms.

Loss

Loss lies on a low spur beside the Menstrie Burn at roughly the centre of the glen, an appropriate location for a house that provided the focus for the management of much of the adjacent area during the 18th century. By the second half of the 18th century it was by far the grandest house in the valley, its status as the residence of a wealthy and influential figure underlined by the emparkment of its surroundings (see pp.25-6). The character of the steading is entirely in keeping with that of the house and, dating to the mid-18th century, it is an early and refined example of an 'improved' farmsteading.

The buildings at Loss were probably demolished before the end of the 19th century, and they are now visible as wall footings ranged around a central courtyard. The house lies along the south side of the yard, a barn on the east, a byre on the west, and what may have been an open-sided shed on the north (fig.32). A kiln-barn is situated immediately outside the north-east angle of the yard, and a garden enclosure extends to the east. The house, which is built of lime-mortared rubble, measures 12m by 4.6m internally, and has a doorway in the centre of the southern wall. There are no partitions remaining, but the fireplaces visible in both ends, and in the middle of the northern side, indicate that the ground-floor was divided into three rooms. Access to the second storey is likely to have been by a timber stair in the central room opposite the front door, though the existence of an external stair is conceivable. An outshot has been butted on to the west end of the house.

Loss came into the Wright family's ownership around 1680.[109] The documentation gives few clues to the form of the house and ancillary buildings at this date, but some of the surviving fabric of the house is of this period. The fireplace in the eastern room, for instance, has finely decorated mouldings and a curved back (fig.32A), and it is likely to date from between about 1680 and 1700. Indeed, the whole of the eastern end of the building is probably of late 17th-century date, and other parts of the fabric, in particular the lower courses of

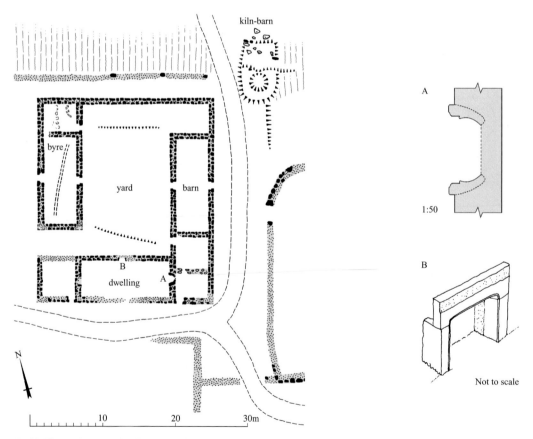

Fig.32 *The strictly rectangular plan (1:500) of the steading at Loss clearly sets it apart from the other stone-built farmsteads in the glen as an 'improved' farm. The late 17th-century fireplace in the east gable (A) probably graced a parlour. The fireplace in the north wall, which has been reconstructed in perspective with its fallen lintel in place, probably dates from refurbishments to the house carried out in the 1750s.*

the walls, may be equally early. Changes in the stonework at the north-east corner suggest that the quoins may have been removed to bond in the steading (below).

In the mid-18th century a more detailed picture of the house and the adjacent steading emerges from the documentary records. The house is referred to in 1744 and early 1745,[110] at which time the steading comprised a stable, byre, barn and kiln. The form and layout of the steading are not mentioned but the roofs were of thatch and all the buildings were in need of repair. A more detailed account of the organisation of the steading is contained in one of the documents, a tack to James Dow in 1744; this reserved '*the western end of the Mansion House of Loss from the Main Partition Wall near the kitchen, the Stable, the two western third parts of the foreyeard, a part of the Barn yard for stacking the said James Wright his victual and liberty to build a barn at and upon the nether end of the corn barn and of drying his victual in the Kiln*'.[111] An inventory from the following year included numerous chairs and lavish furnishing, confirming that this was a gentleman's house of some status.

Extensive renovations were begun in 1750 and continued after Wright's long-planned move to Loss with his wife, Jacobina, in 1753. Prior to this they had been living in his late father-in-law's house in Dunblane.[112] A summary account for expenditure on building work at Loss between 1750 and 1752 comes to a total of over £1000, so this was substantial work.[113] The house, however, was not totally rebuilt; the '*old kitchen windows*', for example, were only repainted. The work undertaken in the house may have included the insertion of the fireplace in the northern wall. The chamfered arrises of this fireplace would not have been out of place in the 1750s (fig.32B). The position of the hearth towards the outer skin of

the wall would have necessitated a projecting chimney stack. Work continued between September 1753 and the summer of 1754, including some demolition work, and extensive drainage and levelling was carried out at the front of the house.[114] Indeed, now that the Wrights were in residence much of this second phase of the renovations was outside, and included work on the byre and stable. A kitchen was also built and there was a new harled yard-dyke. Further work, in August 1755, included the replacement of the kitchen chimney and the harling of the outside of the kitchen and stable. Thus, between about 1750 and 1755 the house appears to have been extensively remodelled.

The documentation provides further clues to the appearance of the building. There is an account for '*painted paper*' for the westernmost room on the first floor, while a further payment was made some time during the 1750s for cleaning snow from the garret. Thus, from these accounts and the surviving ground plan, it can be inferred that at this date the house was a three bay building of two storeys and a garret. On the ground floor, there was a parlour with an ornate fireplace to the east, and the kitchen probably lay at the west end. There is nothing to indicate the arrangement of the stair, but it is likely have been placed more or less centrally, providing access to at least two first-floor rooms and the garret above. The dwelling at Loss, then, was typical of the small lairds' houses introduced about 1700, a style which retained its popularity throughout the 18th century.[115]

It is not entirely clear from the documents if the buildings around the yard were remodelled at this stage, but the surviving fabric appears to be of a piece, and the steading may have been completely rebuilt. The door-openings in the steading are all of mid 18th-century date. An undated sketch

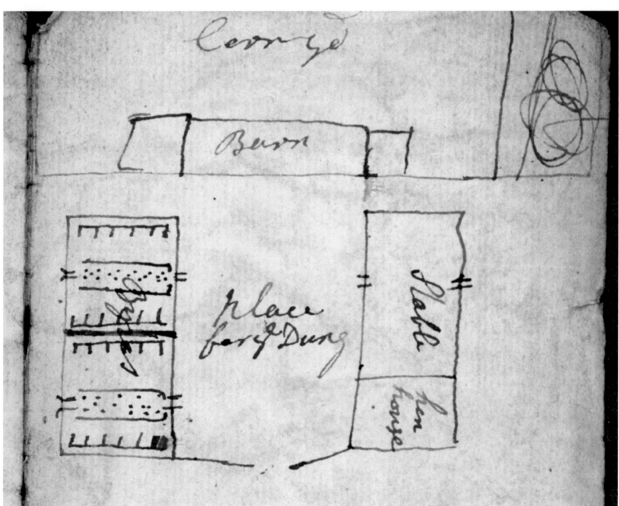

Fig.33 This sketch plan was drawn by James Wright in the early 1750s when he was planning the improvement of his steading at Loss. Reproduced by permission of the Keeper of the Records of Scotland (NAS, RH15/115/5/1, Bundle E).

in Wright's hand on the back of an envelope of a steading (fig.33), presumably dates to this period and represent his plans to rebuild. The dwelling is not shown, but the layout of the buildings is the same as that recorded by the survey (fig.32), with the buildings ranged around a central yard labelled '*place for ye dung*', as is the location of the byre, though the internal arrangement of the byre-drains differs. The stable lies on the east of the yard, and a compartment to the south is labelled '*hen house*'. The sketch also shows a barn along the north side of the yard, in a position approximately corresponding to the platform visible today. A scribble at the top right of the sketch is likely to represent the kiln-barn, while the corn yard shown to the north of the steading lies in what is now very poorly drained ground and this element of the scheme may not have been implemented.

Other accounts deal with relatively minor building work, including the garden, washing green, kiln and stackyard, but, after buying Argyll's Lodging in 1764, Wright spent less time at Loss, and the records of work tail off. After his death in 1769 the documentary sources virtually dry up. A post-nuptial marriage contract, dated 1755, reserved to Jacobina a life rent annuity from the lands of Loss and the life rent use of '*the dining room and two rooms in the west end of the mansion house of Loss, with liberty to her to build a kitchen at the west end of the said mansion house*' if one had not been built by the time of James Wright's death.[116] This may refer to the room abutting the west end of the house, and the right was still reserved to her in 1782,[117] when Loss was leased to John Robb of Jerah. Robb had the use of most of the mansion house, although the dining room and the room above were reserved for the landlord, John Gray.

Loss's grandeur must have declined during the 19th century,

and by 1841 it was occupied only by farm servants.[118] The description in the OS Name Book of 1861 paints a sad picture of '*a one storey farmsteading, un-occupied and partly in ruins*'.[119] By the time of the 2nd edition of the OS 6-inch map, it is completely roofless and derelict.[120]

19th and 20th century buildings

By the 1860s only Jerah and Lipney remained as farmsteads functioning in the glen (fig.35A). Loss had ceased to be a farm before 1813,[121] though it was occupied until the mid-19th century, and Ashentrool, which may have been working as a farm early in the century, was in ruins by 1862-3.[122] Today only Lipney (now known as Dumyat) is still in use as a farm, but little now remains of the mid 19th-century steading.

At Jerah, the mid 19th-century farmhouse and steading stand in ruins (fig.34). The gables of the two-storeyed farmhouse are still standing, but the side walls have largely fallen down. Fireplaces are visible on both floors in each gable, and another may lie amongst the rubble of the north wall. There is a two-phase extension containing the kitchen on the north, and the front door, which was in the south-facing wall, was flanked by windows looking out onto a small garden enclosure. Three further buildings lie around the house. The largest is a long range on the west; it comprises three compartments, the central of which is earlier than the other two. The compartment added to the north is a barn, while the room to the south has nesting boxes for fowl built into the walls, each comprising a recess about 0.4m square. At the north end of the range there is a sheep-dip built of shuttered concrete and iron pickets; water was supplied to the dip by a channel leading from the fields above (fig.35A-C). The second building, the roofless shell of a cart-shed, lies to the east-south-east of the farmhouse, while

Fig.34   By the 1860s, Jerah was the only functioning farmstead left in the glen, and the ruined shell of its mid 19th-century farmhouse, abandoned in the mid 20th-century, can be seen in this ground view taken from the south-west. SC 579459

the third building lies to the south-east of the house; its south end is incorporated into a drystone dyke, and the other three walls are reduced to low grass-grown swellings. What may be the outflow for a drain in the southern wall indicates that this building may have been a byre. A concrete plinth to the north of the farmhouse is all that survives of a kennel. Jerah was abandoned in the 1960s but, as late as 1950, changes were planned to the house and byre.[123]

Although the farmstead described above is the site of the Meikle Jerah referred to in the 17th and 18th centuries,[124] the surviving buildings are essentially those depicted on the 1st edition of the OS 6-inch map dated 1865-6,[125] and there is no trace of any earlier buildings (fig.35A). The form of the surviving buildings suggests a mid-19th-century date for their construction, and they may have been relatively new when Jerah was described in the OS Object Name Book as comprising a two-storey slated farmhouse and single-storey tiled steading.[126] The kennels and the sheep-dip were both added in the 20th century. The Provisional Edition of the OS map of 1951 depicts the farmhouse, the long range and the cart-shed as roofed, and also shows the kennels (fig.35C).[127]

While Jerah and Lipney were the only farmsteads that survived through the 19th century and into the 20th, there was also at least one shepherd's cottage in the glen during the mid to late 19th century. This was the cottage at Red Brae, now a ruin, on the hillside above Jerah, which is shown roofed, with a garden plot, by the OS in 1865-6.[128] The building is a typical three bay, single storey 19th-century cottage with mortared-rubble walls. The south side has been demolished, but it held the entrance, which was probably flanked by two windows. A fireplace and press are visible in the west end. Although no trace of any partition survives, the ground-plan probably conformed to the general pattern of such cottages, with a small central lobby providing access to the rooms on either side, one of which opened on to a small scullery at the rear. A steep ladder-stair in the lobby may have provided access to rooms in the attic. This building was still roofed at the beginning of the 20th century.[129]

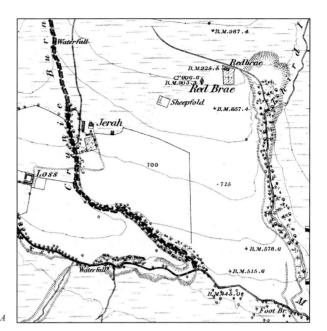

A

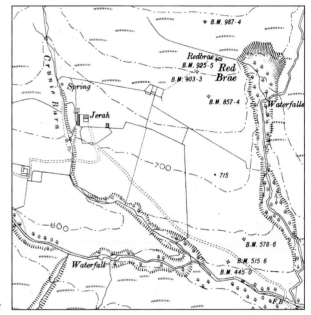

B

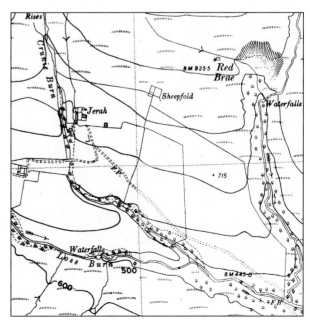

Fig.35   OS 6-inch maps chart the final stages of the withdrawal of settlement from the glen. While Loss was still roofed when the 1st edition map (A) was surveyed in 1855-6,[125] Jerah was the only functioning farmstead, but a shepherd's cottage had been built on Red Brae to the east-north-east. Both Jerah and Red Brae are also shown roofed on the 2nd edition map of 1909,[129] but by then the buildings at Loss were entirely ruinous and are depicted as open rectangles. By the 1950s, only Jerah was occupied, seen here on the 3rd edition map (B),[127] and this too was abandoned in the 1960s.

THE ARCHAEOLOGY OF THE LANDSCAPE

The history of settlement and farming in Menstrie Glen, explored in previous chapters, has shown that the majority of settlement remains probably relate to the late-17th and 18th centuries. This is no less the case for the archaeological remains, such as banks, dykes, rig and mines, formed in the course of land-use, which are found throughout the glen. The recorded history of farming provides a general view of the processes that conditioned life in the glen, particularly in the late 17th and 18th centuries. The dynamism of these processes is also illuminated in detail by the chance survival of documents, showing that the pattern of land-use at any given point was a shifting mosaic of cultivation and pasture. This goes some way towards explaining the complexity of the archaeological remains that survive today. Fossilised cultivation remains occur extensively in Menstrie Glen (e.g. figs 36, 38, 40 and 46-7) and they clearly represent a palimpsest of activity. Because of this complexity, it is difficult to disentangle sequences of land-use that relate to the overall development of settlement and farming from those that reflect changes in repeated cycles

of activity on a year to year basis.

Ploughing is a destructive activity, and the survival of fossilised remains of land-use in the glen is largely as a result of the contraction of arable farming from the hills over the last 240 years. Indeed, the general patterns of survival of field-systems and other cultivation remains in any landscape is conditioned by the intensity and extent of later phases of agriculture. In the case of Menstrie Glen, both the intensity of cultivation and its greatest extent peaked during the 17th and 18th centuries. It is likely, therefore, that the majority of the visible remains, in particular the rig, belong to this period. The only exception of note may be several small groups of cultivation terraces found on the face of the escarpment above Foreside of Lipney, and on the east side of the glen between the escarpment and Little Jerah, which are of earlier date.

Despite the complexity of the remains, a number of broad patterns can be identified in the glen as a whole, reflecting common phases and types of activity. As has been shown, the topography of the glen, with its deeply incised watercourses,

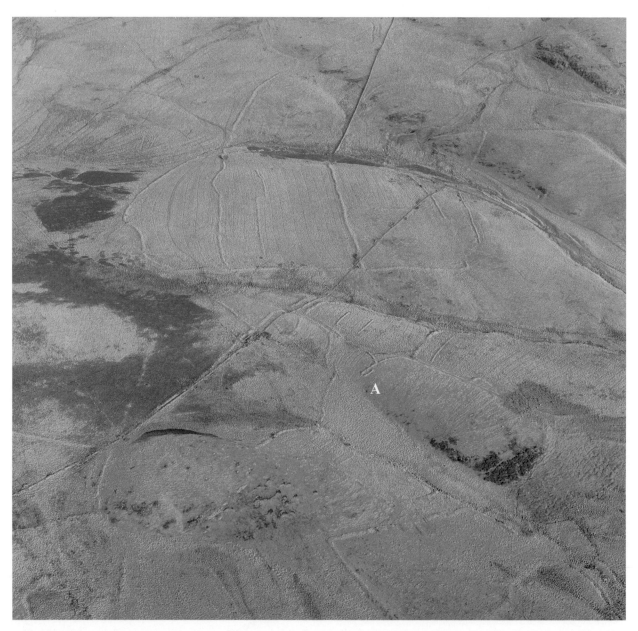

Fig.36   This oblique aerial view from the south-west of the rig and enclosures to the north of Ashentrool reveals a complexity of agricultural remains that is typical of many of the hillsides in Menstrie Glen. This probably reflects repeated cycles of activity over many years, rather than any major changes in land-use, although in this case the stone march-dykes constructed in the 1760s can be seen cutting indiscriminately across the earlier enclosures. The large turf building (A) in the centre has a sunken interior and is possibly the remains of a sheep-house. SC 579454

has fundamentally influenced the disposition of farmsteads and the structure of land-use. The north and east side of the glen is broken up into six, topographically distinct, spurs, which extend from the higher ground towards the valley floor. Each is bounded at its lower end and along it flanks by gorges, while upslope the broad spines of the spurs are crossed by one or more head-dykes. Two of the spurs, those occupied by the farmsteads of Loss and Little Jerah, are examined below. In each case their surviving archaeological remains reflect patterns of use that can be seen more widely across the glen as a whole. In general, three broad zones can be identified, roughly equating to the lower, middle and upper slopes of each spur. The zones are characterised by different suites of land-use remains, reflecting variations in the emphasis of past patterns of farming activity.

The lower slopes are covered by extensive swathes of rig cultivation (fig. 38C), broken only by the gorges dividing up the landscape. In places, areas of rig have been obliterated by 19th- and 20th-century ploughing. Banks are rare, tending only to form major boundaries, and, where they exist, they are frequently overridden by rig. These slopes represent the core of arable ground, with many of the farmsteads disposed along its upper fringe, and they now support the best-quality grazing in the glen.

Situated above the farmsteads and the rig are the middle slopes of the hillsides (fig.38D), which are covered in a patchwork of cultivation remains and enclosures, some of the latter apparently uncultivated. Evidence for the remodelling of the banks and enclosures is common; this suggests an organic process of development, rather than a single conception for the overall pattern of enclosure as it survives today. Enclosures clearly fulfilled a variety of functions, amongst them the folding of stock and the enclosure of arable ground. The majority of rig in the glen is essentially unenclosed, and the most common motivation for building enclosures may have been folding stock to manure future patches of arable, a process called tathing. In many cases patches of rig can be seen to overlie, and to be overlain by, banks; this is likely to

Fig.37 This oblique aerial view looks north-westwards along the upper reaches of Menstrie Glen and, on the right of the image, shows four of the burn gullies that provide natural boundaries to the farms on the east side of the glen. Strathallan can be seen in the distance. SC 579489

reflect a cycle of arable and pastoral use, rather than their use as purely arable field-systems. In the documents there are recurrent references to arable being taken in by Wright in the 1750s (p.21) and, although it is not explicitly stated, this may have involved the construction of boundaries and enclosures. The surviving enclosures vary widely in size, but the smaller examples tend to lie on the lower parts of this zone, while larger enclosures are interspersed with pasture on the higher ground immediately below the head-dykes that mark its upper edge. The head-dykes generally extend across the axis of a spur and frequently display evidence of several phases of construction, bearing witness to the progressive expansion in the extent of enclosed ground.

Beyond the head-dykes lies the hill ground of the uppermost zone (fig.38E), which was exploited for common grazing and peat-cutting. In itself, grazing tends not to have any archaeological manifestation, though the value and importance of grazing rights is evident in the documentation (p.23). However, hollow trackways lead from some farmsteads to the hill, for example at Ashentrool and Little Jerah (p.50), and these may have been formed during the passage of cattle to and from the pastures in the manner detailed by Wright at Tounhead (p.23). The only other archaeological manifestations of grazing are shielings (p.30), which formed part of an earlier system of transhumant exploitation of the upland grazing for cattle and sheep during the summer months. Sixteen groups of shieling-huts are situated in the middle and upper zones in the glen and its side valleys (p.31, fig.23), generally in areas of relatively good, sheltered grazing. Those in the middle zone were evidently subsumed by the expansion of settlement and agriculture in the late 17th and early 18th centuries, but it is not known when the practice died out. The upper zone also contains the majority of the peat deposits in the glen, blanketing the hilltops and filling some small basins. Peat was a valuable resource that is likely to have been exploited for fuel from a very early date, and evidence of peat cutting can still be seen on many of the hills.

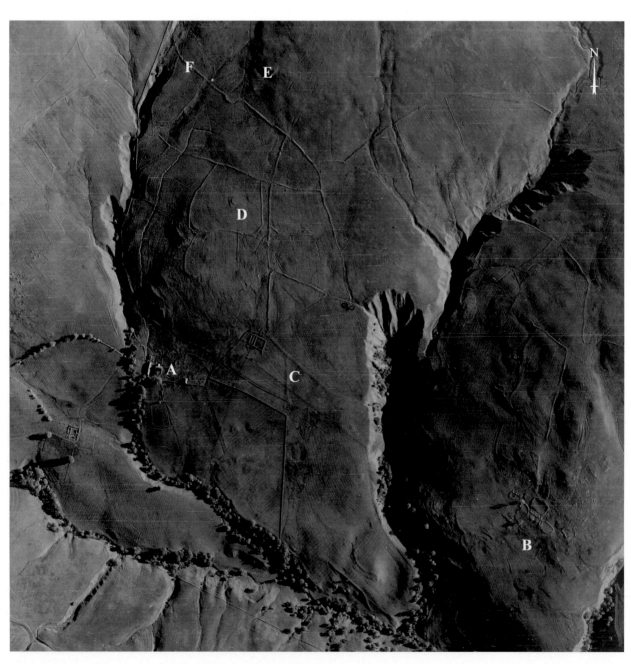

Fig.38 Three broad zones can be detected in the pattern of surviving archaeological remains, illustrated here by this vertical aerial photograph of Jerah (A) and Little Jerah (B), which occupy spurs on the north-east side of the glen. The lowest zone (C), at the bottom of the picture below the farmsteads, is covered with blocks of rig, while the middle zone (D) is represented by a patchwork of rig and enclosures between the farmsteads and the head-dykes. The uppermost zone (E) is represented by the rough pastures on the higher slopes beyond the head-dykes (F). (106G/SCOT/UK120 20 June 1946, 3114). SC 579462.

The Landscape

The surviving agricultural remains in the landscape include various categories of evidence i.e. rig-and-furrow, cultivation terraces, head-dykes, fields, enclosures, fencing, march-dykes, and sheep-houses. These are discussed separately in sections that examine both the archaeological and historical evidence from the glen. To focus on each category of evidence in turn, however, is to risk divorcing the remains from the landscape itself. By-and-large, the practices represented by these remains operated as part of an agricultural system, albeit one that was immensely flexible and capable of rapid change. Therefore, land-use remains should also be considered in concert. To this end, three areas are described and discussed initially, the first on the west side of the glen, covering the area of the Lipneys, and the other two on the north and east of the glen – Loss and Little Jerah respectively (fig.39).

These areas show that the three broad zones outlined above do not have hard and fast boundaries. In the first instance, the zones are based upon the patterns of surviving evidence, but they also reflect the ways in which each zone was used, particularly at the point when settlement had reached its fullest extent immediately before the dramatic contraction of the mid-18th century. Agricultural practices were evidently fluid, not only responding to the exigencies of farming life on daily and yearly cycles, but also to the trends in the expansion and contraction of settlement.

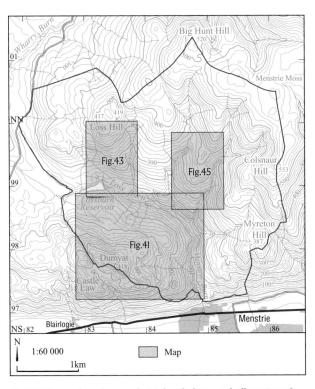

Fig.39 This map shows the areas depicted on the larger scale illustrations of Lipney, Loss and Little Jerah.

Lipney is the largest area dealt with in this section. It covers an area that has already figured in the discussions of the expansion of settlement into the glen, the character of the settlements themselves, and also in the farming systems that were being practised. Some of this evidence is repeated, but only in so far as it is necessary to illustrate the combination of archaeological and documentary evidence that has been recovered and the changing patterns of farm organisation that they chart. At Loss, the documentary sources illuminate the archaeological remains, but in a rather different landscape that displays the impact of an improving landlord and the emparkment of the environs of his house. By way of contrast, the third example, Little Jerah, on the east side of the glen, is drawn from an area for which there are few documentary sources, and any analysis of the history of its land-use rests largely upon the archaeological survey.

Lipney

The property of Lipney, taking in the north and east flanks of Dumyat, was one of the medieval holdings in Menstrie Glen, and, as we have seen (p.19), the emergence of its three farms, namely Foreside, Quarterside and Backside, is likely to reflect the expansion of settlement into the glen during the 16th and 17th centuries. A tenant of Backside is documented in the 1690s and, during the early 18th century, all three farms were distinct possessions. After 1730, however, the lease of Quarterside appears to have been combined with one of the other two, and by the early 19th century Lipney was a single tenancy. In addition to the main farmsteads, the archaeological survey has revealed at least six turf-walled byre-houses on Lipney. The majority are undocumented, but one may be the farmstead known as Cadger Knowes (p.32, fig.24), lying at the west end of the area illustrated (fig.41), which was occupied in the 1750s. While the others may be undocumented survivals of a late 17th-century settlement pattern, it is more likely that they are 18th-century farmsteads (pp.32-3). Clusters of huts recorded along the flanks of Dumyat, however, probably date from before the 18th century, in this case reflecting a medieval pattern of shieling (pp.30-1).

The management of the holdings in the first half of the 18th century is relatively well-documented. Its overriding characteristic appears to have been flexibility, illustrated by the various tacks surviving from the period between 1730 and 1752. In 1730 Donald McFarlane in Backside and Andrew Roy in Foreside had taken Lipney jointly, without distinguishing their rights to particular parts.[130] Two years later, however, they agreed that McFarlane would take Backside and Middlequarter (presumably Quarterside), and Roy would take Foreside and the mansion house that stood there. Each would be liable for his proportion of the taxes, while the hill above the head-dyke was to be held in common. Subsequently, in 1740, Roy took Foreside, part of Quarterside, half the hill and his share of the taxes,[131] while James McFarlane took Backside and part of Quarterside named Greens of Craigneish. In 1752 Foreside was set to Andrew Roy, and Backside had passed to Robert Dow.[132] In each of these tacks there are variations in the minor terms, forming part of a continuous series of adjustments, and by 1752 Quarterside seems to have been thought of as part of Foreside. Throughout this time the agreements assume that the two tenants would labour together from time to time, sharing the work equally on the ground named White Meadows and Greens of Craigneish; otherwise these areas were to be common grazing (p.17).

The greater part of the surviving archaeological remains almost certainly relate to the period covered by the tacks outlined above; they occupy a broad gently-sloping terrace, bounded on the north and east by the steeply incised gully of the Menstrie Burn. The back of the terrace is marked by an irregular break of slope, giving way to the rapidly quickening slopes of Dumyat. The majority of the cultivated ground is delimited by the uppermost of what is probably a succession of head-dykes. These take in the gentler slopes up to 250m OD on the east flank of Dumyat, and extend roughly along the line of the break of slope on the north flank, pulling away from it to the south-east of Backside to avoid an area of relatively poor ground. The three zones that were defined in the introduction to this section (lower, middle and upper) are most clearly visible on the east flank of Dumyat. On the northern flank of the hill, the middle zone, comprising a patchwork of enclosures, rig and pasture, is apparently missing, and the head-dyke essentially divides the rigs on the lower slope from the hill pastures. The existence of the head-dyke, however, has not precluded cultivation on the hill pastures, as the surviving patches of rig and various farmsteads demonstrate. These rigs are poorly formed and are likely to represent only short-lived episodes of cultivation, as is implied by a tack of 1740 for Foreside and Quarterside of Lipney. This stipulated that the use of the land for cultivation and pasture should be alternated in three year breaks.[133]

The pattern of archaeological remains on Lipney, however, is evidently cumulative, and this goes some way towards explaining the disposition of features along the north side of the hill. The uppermost line of the head-dyke is that recorded in the tacks of 1740, which describe its course in detail: '*the old head dyke above Tom Lochie, leading from the Warro Bank to the Ston Hill of Lipnoch and from thence to the Kings High Way leading to the Back Side House of Lipnoch and from thence to the Kirk Ford on the west end of Lipnoch ground, laying next to the muir of Fossackie*'.[134] Around Quarterside, however, the dyke exhibits several phases of construction, some representing small adjustments to its line, while others demonstrate the incorporation of the lines of earlier banks, such as can be detected in the dislocation of its line on the north-east flank of Ston Hill. The farmstead on the south-east of Ston Hill also pre-dates the construction of two phases of the head-dyke, the earlier of which cuts across the south-east flank of Ston Hill, while the later runs along the ridge at right-angles and extends to Backside of Lipney. This was not the only line adopted for a head-dyke, however, and what is probably an earlier line bounds the intensively cultivated ground north of Quarterside. Like the upper dyke, it also appears to incorporate the boundary of at least one earlier enclosure and cuts across others; close by them is another turf-built byre-house, which would originally have lain outside its line.

The evidence for multi-period construction in the head-dykes, discrete earlier enclosures and farmsteads, as well as contemporary fields and farmsteads lying beyond the dykes, reveals the sequence by which settlement expanded and new land was progressively taken in hand. Some of the fields lying in the zone on the middle slopes almost certainly began life in the hill pastures of the uppermost zone, as did some of the smaller farmsteads. The choice of site for these new fields and farmsteads was probably guided by the earlier pattern of shieling activity on the hills, with its enhancement of the fertility of discrete areas of ground. It should also be borne in mind that landlords were maintaining their shieling rights through the 17th century as a ploy in the assertion of their claim to property rights. Such considerations may also have dictated the locations of new farmsteads. But for the contraction of settlement in the mid-18th century, it is more than likely that the farmstead and cultivation remains at Cadger Knowes, and those at several other locations above Backside of Lipney, would similarly have been taken in by a head-dyke. When the head-dyke was extended north-westwards from Quarterside to Backside, the ground below the earlier line to the north of Quarterside became the focus for intensive cultivation, eradicating most of the earlier enclosures, the presence of which is indicated by discontinuous lengths of bank on this part of the hillside.

Implicit in this analysis of the archaeological remains is that the head-dykes are not the earliest elements to be constructed in this part of the farming landscape. It can also be surmised that the broad zoning of the remains in the landscape is a product of the way in which the extent of arable land within the head-dykes expanded, coupled with the intensity of the cultivation that subsequently took place on the lower slopes. In effect, as the extent of cultivation expanded, any traces of enclosures on the lower slopes are likely to have been removed. Most of the rig is defined by shallow, closely-spaced grooves, reflecting cultivation during the first half of the 18th century (pp.52-3), and, aside from the head-dyke, it is largely unenclosed. Some of the rig is so ephemeral that it is visible only on aerial photographs and may represent single episodes of ploughing. Not all the cultivation remains are of this date, however, and small areas continued in cultivation into the 19th century. An early 19th-century map depicts areas of arable to the east of Backside and beside Quarterside,[135] and in these areas there are straight, shallow furrows overlying the earlier curved rigs. Many of the fragmentary banks and enclosures scattered across the hillsides below the head-dykes are, as we have seen, likely to belong to earlier arrangements of the pasture and arable, but others may be broadly contemporary with the head-dykes, and have been reduced to their present fragmentary state by repeated cycles of tathing and cultivation. The enclosures used in this way are betrayed by traces of low rig, but in some cases, in particular on the hillside west of Quarterside, the banks appear to enclose only grazing land. At least one of the latter enclosures overlies the head-dyke described in 1740, but another is crossed by it, again revealing the complexity of the management practices in operation.

By the 18th century, and possibly for some time before then, the head-dykes were a fundamental element in the articulation of this landscape. Head-dykes clearly bounded the upper limit of the intensively cultivated ground, but they also enclosed pastures. The documentary sources demonstrate that cycles of grazing and arable were an important element in managing soil nutrition below the head-dykes, but similar practices were almost certainly equally important in the arrangements of earlier enclosures before their construction. Tathing and other forms of manure management were vital to the success or failure of the crops that were sown in these plots. The value of sheep manure was probably a consideration in the housing of sheep recorded in documentary sources at Foreside and Backside. It is also possible that some of the larger buildings amongst the shieling groups on the north side of Dumyat are sheep-houses, constructed on the best pastures as part of their later management (pp.59-60).

The final elements of this landscape worth noting are the enclosures that extend along the south-west bank of the Menstrie Burn. Comprising turf banks with external stone faces, these boundaries are amongst the latest elements in the sequence of enclosure, and are notable for their straightness and the regularity of the enclosures they form. From the 1750s Wright planted large numbers of trees (pp.25-6), and these enclosures along the Menstrie Burn probably defined his plantations. The documents (p.56) refer to fences, although no trace of them survives.

Fig.40 In this ground view taken from the north the broad curving grooves of the rig on the slope to the north of Quarterside are thrown into high relief by the late afternoon sunshine. SC 579476

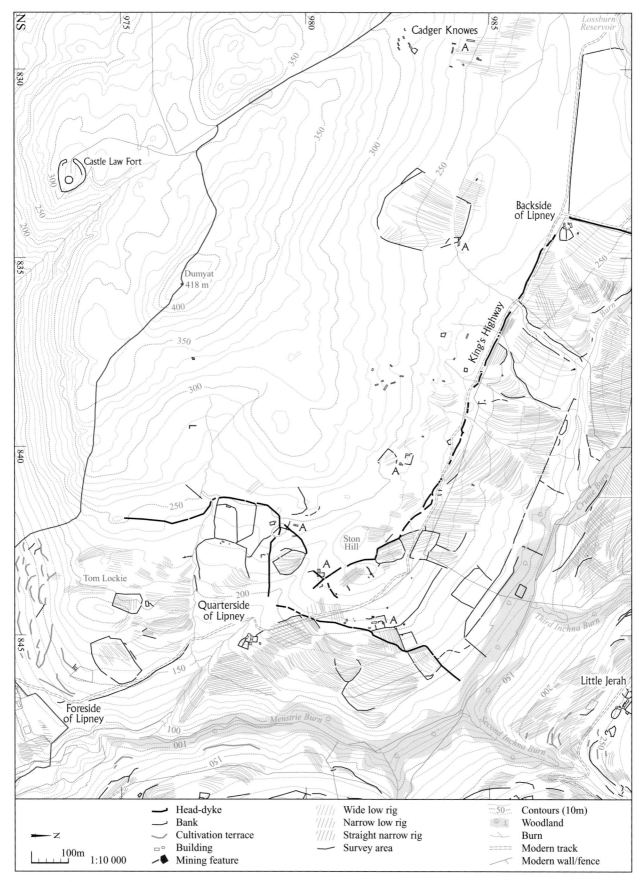

Fig.41 *This map of the farm of Lipney illustrates the complex and cumulative character of the archaeological remains extending round the eastern and northern flanks of Dumyat. Of particular note are the head-dykes, which evidently represent several phases of construction and appear to be among the later components of the remains. While the main 18th-century farms of Foreside, Quarterside and Backside are stone-built, there is a series of turf byre-houses, identified by the letter A, which all lie beyond the head-dykes, usually adjacent to ephemeral traces of rig. Rather than representing an earlier phase of settlement, these byre-houses appear to be the dwellings of minor tenants, in at least one case dating from the mid-18th century.*

Loss

The south-facing spur dropping down from Loss Hill to the site of Wright's house at Loss is one of a series of naturally defined blocks of land on the north side of the Menstrie Burn (fig.43). In this sense it is more typical of the topography of the glen than the ground occupied by the Lipneys. Its south-facing slopes are also amongst the more favourable locations for agriculture. It is, therefore, one of the prime positions for settlement in the glen, contrasting with the north- and east-facing slopes occupied by Quarterside and Backside. On these grounds alone, it can hardly be a surprise that Loss should have emerged as the hub of the estate taking in the west side of Menstrie Glen, and the centre for a large cattle and sheep raising business in the 18th century.

The character of the archaeological remains on the spur conform to the three zones identified earlier (pp.42-4), but they are heavily skewed here by the impact of James Wright's improvements on the lower slopes around his house. Not only are the boundaries constructed around the house recorded in detail in Wright's notes (pp.25-6 and 56), but the majority of the cultivation remains within them comprise closely-spaced straight grooves, in one place overlying traces of curved rigs. The emparkment of the lower slopes and the cultivation of the enclosed ground in the 19th century have effectively removed from this zone the physical evidence of cultivation and land-use predating 1760.

The slopes above Loss display a complex pattern of fragmentary enclosures and extensive cultivation remains, and they typify the character of the remains found on the middle slopes – a similar pattern will also be seen in the case of Little Jerah. As at Lipney, the head-dyke is evidently multi-period, following three separate lines along the contour towards the north-east, but it is by no means certain that in this instance they incorporate any earlier banks or enclosures. The sequence of their construction is not clear on the ground, but the lowest of the three head-dykes appears to be the latest, even though it cannot be traced all the way across the spur. These head-dykes post-date a further head-dyke which extends across the face of the spur from north-west to south-east. Most of the ground it encloses on Loss Hill has always been rough pasture, but the ground on Ashentrool to the west has been extensively cultivated.

As far as can be seen from the documentary record, during the first half of the 18th century these slopes were used largely for growing oats, with barley being restricted to the better ground around the steading. Most of the rig comprises closely-spaced shallow grooves, much of it gently curving on plan. There is also at least one plot of widely-spaced curving grooves below the head-dyke on the west flank of the spur, and several patches of broad rigs with raised crowns on the east flank, between the head-dyke and the west bank of the Crunie Burn. As at Lipney, the rig defined by close-set grooves can probably be attributed to the years before the 1760s, but the other types of rig may also have remained in cultivation until this time. Nevertheless, the chaotic arrangement of the fragmentary banks and enclosures, and the interdigitating blocks of rig, indicate again that the pattern of the remains in this zone is cumulative, and probably represents a considerable period of activity. The fertility of these slopes was probably maintained mainly by tathing, which, carried out over many years, may explain the pattern that has been recorded in the survey. One of only two sheep-houses that have been identified in the glen (pp.59-60) is sited at the foot of the enclosures on this slope. This would also have provided a convenient source of manure to be spread on the adjacent arable.

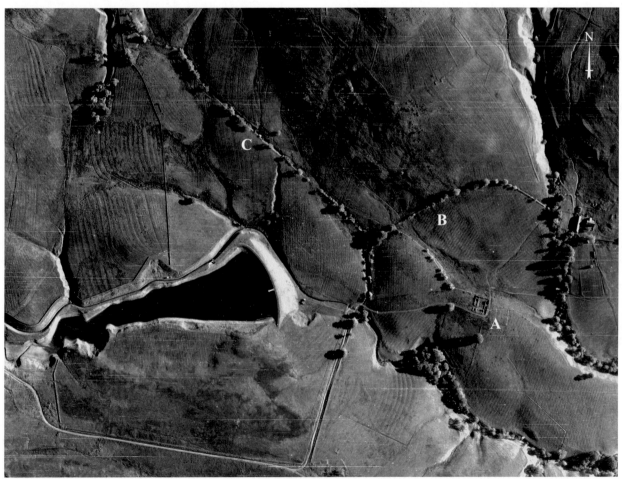

Fig.42 The area of emparked policies that James Wright created around his house and steading at Loss can be seen in this vertical aerial photograph. The steading (A) is visible centre right, with the tree-lined park boundary (B) built in 1758 arcing around the north, and the boundary (C) added in 1762 extending away to the north-west. (106G/SCOT/UK120, 20 June 1946, 3113). SC 579452

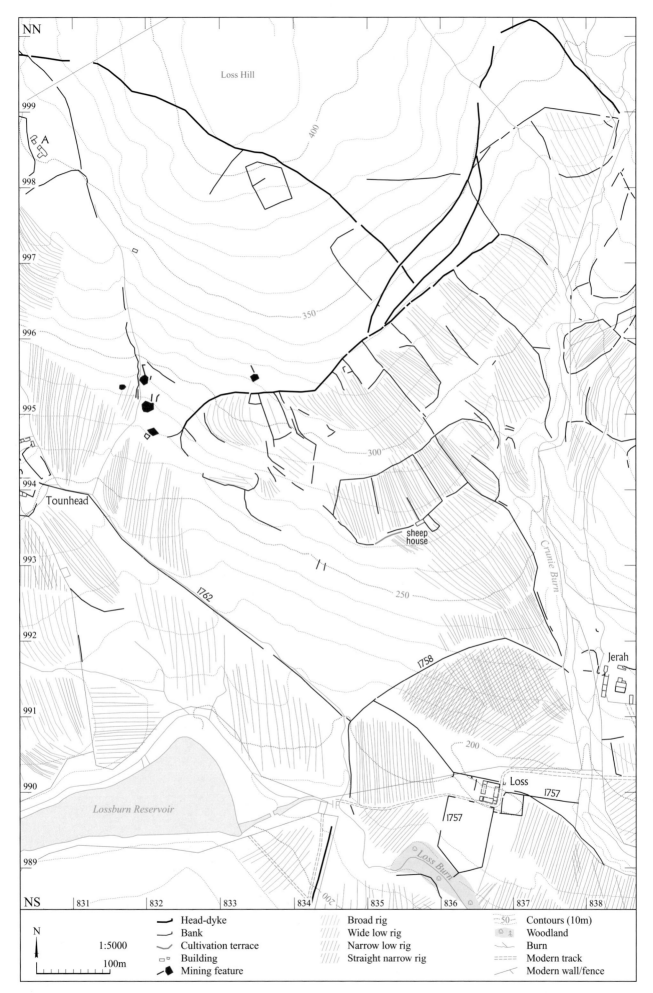

Loss Hill

999

A

998

997

996

350

995

300

994

Tounhead

993

1762

250

sheep
house

Crunie Burn

992

1758

Jerah

991

200

990

Loss

1757

Lossburn Reservoir

1757

Loss Burn

989

NS   831   832   833   834   00c   835   836   837   838

N	⎯ Head-dyke	///// Broad rig	┈50┈ Contours (10m)
	⌐ Bank	///// Wide low rig	Woodland
1:5000	⌣ Cultivation terrace	///// Narrow low rig	Burn
100m	▭ Building	///// Straight narrow rig	═══ Modern track
	◆ Mining feature		Modern wall/fence

Fig.43 The archaeological remains on this spur on the north side of the glen represent several phases of construction, illustrated by the head-dyke in the centre which follows at least three separate lines. The enclosures on the lower ground around the steading at Loss were built in 1757, and the larger enclosures in 1758 and 1762, as part of James Wright's reorganisation of the glen into an extensive sheepwalk.

49

Little Jerah

The spur between the Second and Third Inchna Burns is even more sharply defined than that at Loss, the steep gullies along its flanks forming formidable topographical boundaries (fig.45). Unlike Loss, however, there are no visible signs of improvement, and the agricultural remains have survived undisturbed since the farm reverted to a sheep walk and the steading was abandoned, probably by the late 18th century. The spur lends itself to the division into the zones that have been proposed, and their character is more precisely drawn here than in the other examples that have been presented. As can be seen from the plan, the farmstead of Little Jerah, which is also known as Easter Jerah, is situated at the boundary between the lower and middle slopes of the spur. The ground below is swathed in rig, while that above carries a patchwork of rig, enclosures and rough pasture, extending up to the lower of the two head-dykes. Adjacent to the upper head-dyke there is a sheep bucht, one of only four identified in the glen (p.58), while on the slope above the Second Inchna Burn, beyond the dyke, there is a cluster of shieling huts (p.30).

The farmstead is stone-built (p.34) and comprises at least three buildings, a possible fourth being represented by a small irregular footing on the upslope side. Two of the buildings are ranged along the contour, and the third is set at right-angles to them on the downslope side. Of the former, the westernmost has three compartments and the other four. In each of the three buildings there is clear evidence for distinct phases of addition to the buildings, rather than a single build. One of the compartments in each of the three buildings is a byre, and there is a midden hollow outside the entrance of the western building. Three enclosures in the immediate vicinity of the buildings appear to have been garden plots, while two to the south-east may have been folds for stock.

The history of the farm is poorly documented and the date at which the farmstead was abandoned is not known for certain. It is a reasonably safe assumption, however, that the history of settlement here broadly follows the pattern established on Wright's holdings (p.26), with steadings abandoned during the 1760s and 1770s. The OS 6-inch map of 1865-6 does not depict any buildings at this location,[136] and it was evidently long deserted by then.

The main expanse of rig, presumably representing the most intensively cultivated areas on the spur, lies in a band that sweeps north-westwards off the relatively steep ground to the south of the farmstead to the gentler slopes above the Third Inchna Burn. The rigs form distinct blocks (furlongs), in places interdigitating, and the lower edge of some of the blocks is sometimes marked by a substantial lynchet . These lynchets are not to be confused with the cultivation terraces lying to the south-east of the farmstead, which probably date from an earlier phase of cultivation on the spur (p.54). The majority of the rig is characterised by the type of closely-spaced shallow grooves (see pp.52-3) that have been encountered already at Loss and Lipney, and is probably also of 18th-century date. Here too, however, there are patches of widely-spaced grooves, situated at the upper edge of the cultivated ground on the north-west and south-east flanks of the spur respectively. The north-west patch lies within an enclosure immediately below the head-dyke, which is one of a series of enclosures recorded in various states of completeness on this side of the spur.

The contrast between the remains on either side of the spur is striking, the enclosures on the north-west displaying the evidence of repeated remodelling that we have seen at Loss and Lipney. Again, the practice of tathing offers the most likely explanation for the complexity, although there is also a strong impression that the larger blocks of rig have encroached upon the area that forms the focus of these enclosures. The large enclosures on the south-east flank of the hill, which overlie several blocks of rig (one of the blocks being of widely-spaced grooves), were also probably temporary folds created in the course of tathing. They exhibit at least two phases of construction, which were probably separated by episodes of cultivation.

The multi-period construction of the head-dykes at Loss and Lipney is also evident at Little Jerah. Here it takes a slightly different form, however, the better preservation of the upper head-dyke suggesting that it is of later date than the lower dyke. The irregular course of the lower head-dyke may also hint at a similar process to that found at Lipney, where the line of the dyke evidently took in the boundaries of a number of earlier enclosures. At Little Jerah the evidence is by no means so clear cut, but there is a strong possibility that the western half of its course incorporates an earlier boundary that extended along the top of fields occupying the slope below. The eastern stretch of the head-dyke follows a direct route across to the gully of the Second Inchna Burn, and midway along this sector the boundary of a further intake butts against it. It is not known whether this intake belongs to the process of expansion that lead to the construction of the new head-dyke, or whether it relates to subsequent land-use within the newly enclosed ground. Fragments of a similar intake can be seen on the west side of the spur, although in that case there is no visible junction with the lower head-dyke, and the sequence of their construction is uncertain.

The complexity of the inter-relationships between arable land and pasture is perhaps clearer at Little Jerah than in either of the other cases that have been presented. A significant proportion of the ground below the lower head-dyke has never been cultivated, most of it lying on the thin soils and rock outcrops along the spine of the spur to the north-east of the farmstead, and this has always been given over to grazing. Furthermore, the repeated overprinting of enclosures and cultivation remains on these slopes almost certainly reflects the practice of tathing. The archaeological remains have also preserved another aspect of this relationship, represented by the braided hollow trackways (depicted in outline on fig.45) that ascend the spine of the spur, evidently heading for a gap in the upper head-dyke. These may have been formed as a result of the movement of stock between the farmstead and the common grazings, as well as from the transport of peat down from the higher ground.

Fig.44 The farmstead in this oblique aerial view from the north-west is almost certainly Little Jerah. The stone buildings are clearly visible, as are its associated enclosures, and the steep gully that forms the eastern boundary of the farm can be seen in the background. SC 579486

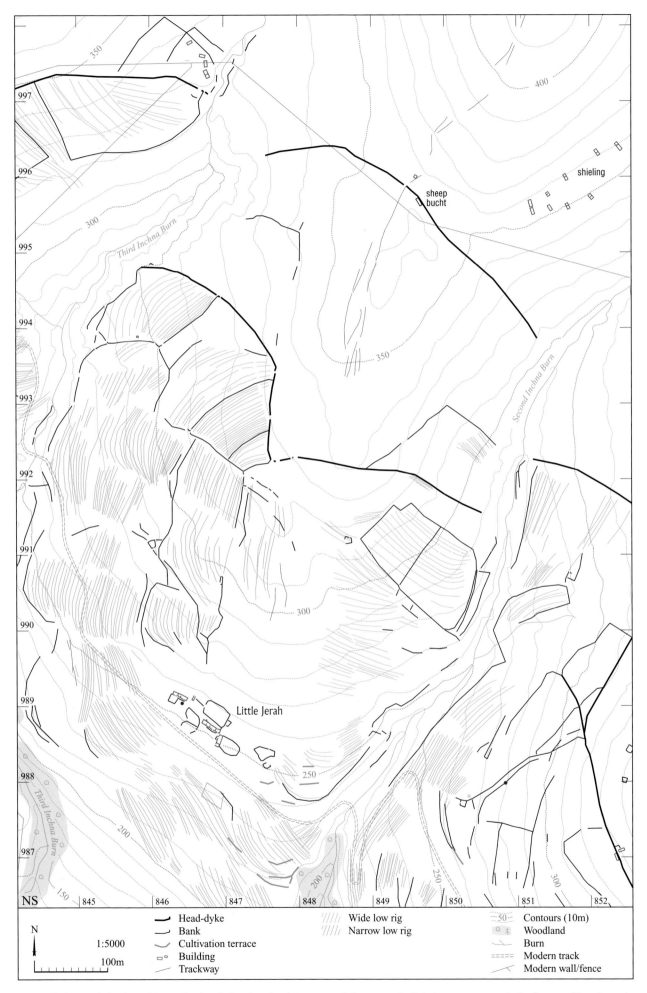

Fig.45 The farmstead of Little Jerah lies on the edge of a broad swathe of rigs covering the lower ground, which gives way to a network of enclosures, cultivated ground and grazing, with two phases of head-dyke beyond. These remains are a manifestation of the complex inter-relationships between arable and pasture, almost certainly including tathing.

51

The Components of the Landscape

The three areas that have been examined at Lipney, Loss and Little Jerah, provide detailed examples of the disposition of archaeological evidence in the landscape. This evidence can be broken down into a series of separate categories, which in the following sections is combined with historical sources drawn from throughout the glen. These give further insights into the practices that lay behind the creation of the surviving remains, and highlight the significance of the remarkable documentation contained in Wright's papers. The sections lead with rig, the most extensive of the archaeological remains, covering large swathes of the lower and middle reaches of the glen (fig.48). Subsequent sections deal with: cultivation terraces, which may have a medieval or earlier origin; head-dykes; enclosures of various types and fences; march boundaries; sheep-houses; and finally mining remains.

Rig

The hillsides of Menstrie Glen are covered with a palimpsest of rig, relatively little of which is easy to see on the ground. Low slanting sunlight and a distant view may throw even the slightest rigs into high relief, but the full extent and patterning of rigs are most clearly appreciated from aerial photographs taken in the 1940s (e.g. figs.46,47). These date from before the most recent episodes of ploughing for reseeded pasture and the small-scale forestry plantations, which have obscured some of the cultivation remains. As a result of the archaeological survey four types of rig have been identified in the glen:

- **Broad rig**: broad, sinuous rig with high crowns, measuring 8m-12m between furrows and up to 1m in height (fig.46A);
- **Wide low rig**: defined by widely-spaced, sinuous grooves set between 5m and 8m apart (fig.47C);
- **Narrow low rig**: defined by closely-spaced, sinuous groves set about 3m apart (fig.47B);
- **Straight narrow rig**: defined by closely-spaced straight grooves set about 4m apart (fig.47A).

The areas of broad rig within the survey area are the most limited in extent, with discrete patches occurring beside the Crunie and Loss Burns, as well as near Ashentrool (fig.46). The rigs display the shape of a reverse-S on plan and are thought to have been formed by the use of a fixed mould-board plough set to turn the sod inwards. While the dating of this sort of rig is poorly defined, its origins go back into the medieval period.[137] There is no direct dating for the broad rig in Menstrie Glen, but the discrete patches that are visible may be no more than fragments of much more extensive rig-systems that were truncated by other forms of cultivation during the 18th century. Where there are stratigraphic relationships with banks or other forms of rig, the broad rig is consistently the earlier. Indeed, in 1755 and 1756 Wright records the obliteration of the old 'furrs' at Little Loss,[138] though it must be admitted that there is no indication of the character of those rigs, and they may even have been headlands between blocks of ploughed land. While it can be argued that the formation of broad rig is relatively early in the glen, it is clear that the surviving patches continued to be cultivated throughout the 18th century, and did not become fossilised until at least 1760.

The two types of rig defined by sinuous shallow grooves – wide low rig and narrow low rig – may be variations of the same basic form of cultivation, the narrower spacing between furrows a product of splitting wide low rigs with an intermediate furrow. This can be seen in places above Jerah (fig.47), where there is an alternating pattern of deep and shallow furrows, the latter presumably splitting wide rigs defined by the deeper furrows. Elsewhere on Jerah there is no discernible evidence that the closely-spaced furrows have evolved from wider rigs, though in places the intensity of ploughing may have obliterated all trace of any earlier phase of cultivation. Indeed, the furrows of the wide low rig occur

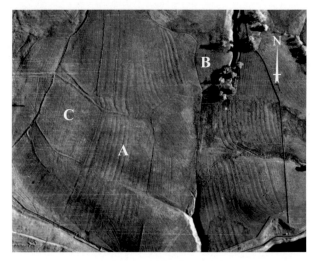

Fig.46   This vertical aerial photograph (106G/SWT/UK120 20 June 1946, 4048) shows the broad rig (A) in the vicinity of Ashentrool (B). Narrow rig (C), defined by closely-spaced sinuous grooves, can also be seen, together with elements of several enclosures. SC 611345

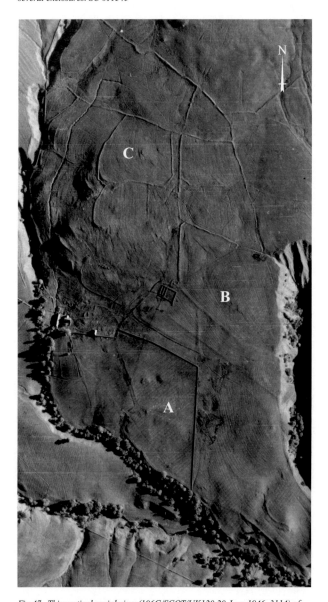

Fig.47   This vertical aerial view (106G/SCOT/UK120 20 June 1946, 3114) of the hillside around Jerah displays at least three of the different types of rig that have been recorded in Menstrie Glen. On the lower slopes close to the farm straight narrow rig (A) can be seen, but moving up the picture blocks of sinuous narrow rig (B) can be seen. Further up the spur, in the enclosures below the head-dykes, there are several patches of wide low rig (C) defined by shallow, curving grooves. SC 611377

only in discrete patches in the glen (fig.48) in a pattern of survival reminiscent of the broad rig; this may suggest that they belonged to more extensive rig-systems truncated by the ploughing that produced the narrow sinuous grooves. The plots of wide low rig do not disrupt any banks, nor do they overlie other narrow rigs, thus indicating a place in the sequence of rig types in the glen that is earlier rather than later. In contrast, the systems of closely-spaced grooves forming narrow low rigs, not only often overlie banks, but are also the most extensive type of rig in the glen. As such, they almost certainly represent the main form of cultivation on the eve of the improvements,

and the mention of rigs throughout Wright's records of sowing (p.21) are generally likely to refer to this type of rig.

Straight narrow rigs, defined by closely-spaced straight grooves, are confined to those areas into which arable cultivation contracted during the late-18th and 19th centuries (see p.28, fig.21). They may have been formed by the lighter swing ploughs that were introduced in the late 18th century.[139] Where there is any visible sequence with other land-use remains, these rigs are clearly later, and were only superseded by forms of improved cultivation in which field-surfaces were entirely smooth and display no grooves. The necessity

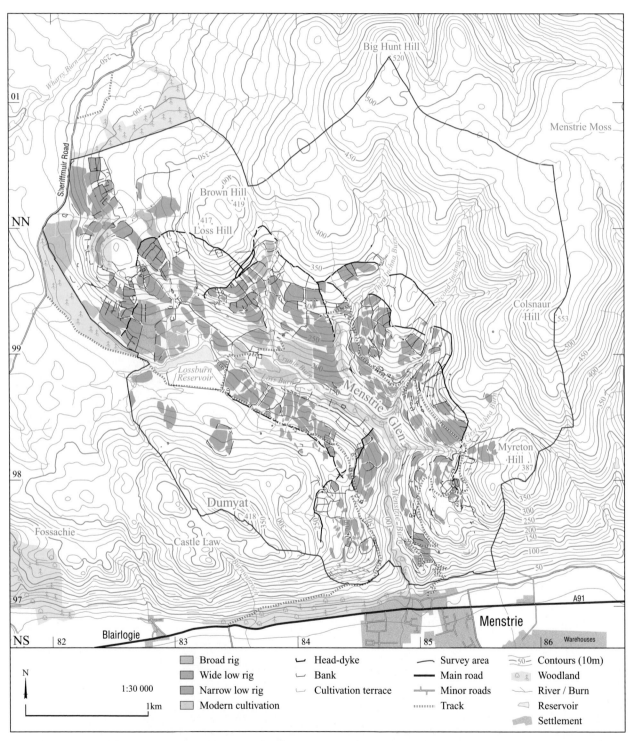

Fig.48 This map shows the extents of the different types of rig recorded in the glen, as well as remains of the enclosures and head-dykes associated with them. Together, they give an overall impression of the maximum extent of farming activity throughout Menstrie Glen in the mid-18th century, but the different types of rig also broadly reflect the contraction of cultivation that has taken place. The broad, high-crowned blocks of rig, some of which are known to have been in use in the first half of the 18th century, tend to lie at the periphery of the overall area under cultivation, as do the patches of wide low rig. In contrast, the narrow low rig is far more extensive, occupying many of the lower slopes, and almost certainly represents the main areas under cultivation on the eve of the Improvements. Late 18th and 19th century cultivation is entirely restricted to the lower slopes around Loss and Jerah.

for furrows to improve drainage of fields receded with the widespread adoption of underground drains during the 19th century. Patches of smooth field-surfaces around Jerah, for example (fig.47), have almost certainly been drained and correspond broadly with ground marked as arable on the 1st edition of the OS map (p.41, fig.35).[140] Cultivation in the late-19th and 20th centuries was limited to those areas and continued to contract.

The change in the morphology of the cultivation remains may correspond to the introduction of light swing ploughs. This may also have coincided with the abandonment of oxen, which are commonly recorded in 17th century inventories, for traction, whereas 18th century tacks assume that horses will be employed for ploughing, muck spreading, harrowing and other feudal duties demanded of tenants (e.g. fig.17).[141]

Cultivation terraces
The intensity of post-medieval cultivation has severely curtailed the potential for any earlier agricultural remains to survive on the lower slopes of the glen. There are, however, four groups of terraces that appear to have been formed in the course of earlier cultivation. These are part of a much wider distribution of terracing in the Ochils.[142]

Cultivation terraces can be formed by ploughing at any period, a natural consequence of soil movement on slopes when the surface vegetation cover has been broken. The soil catches on obstacles on the slope, in this case the lower edge of the field or plot, where a terrace will develop as soil from successive ploughings washes downslope; conversely, the upper edge of the field is marked by a step etched into the slope by the loss of soil downslope. In the case of rig lying along the contour, an unploughed baulk between each rig or furlong would act as an obstacle to soil movement, leading to the accumulation of soil against the baulk forming the lower edge of each rig. This type of terracing has already been encountered at Little Jerah (p.50) and is present elsewhere in the Ochils, but it is clearly a form of rig and has been treated here as such. In other cases a terrace may have been created deliberately by the construction of a baulk, perhaps of field-gathered stones, and the deposition of soil from elsewhere on its upslope sides to form a level plot. It is this type of terracing that has been identified as a survival of earlier cultivation in the glen.

Typically, this terracing comprises a marked scarp or break of slope along its leading edge, which may incorporate traces of a retaining bank of stones; behind the scarp, the terrace forms a level platform, which is cut back into the slope at the rear. Each terrace tends to be discrete, lying on broken ground that is otherwise marginal for cultivation. These examples, therefore, were probably formed at a time when there was already extensive exploitation of the better soils in the glen. At first sight this might indicate that they are of 17th- or 18th-century date, but in two cases, on the north banks of both the First and Second Inchna Burns, the terraces are overlain by rig, which sweeps down across them at an oblique angle. As a group, therefore, it may be postulated that the Menstrie Glen terraces predate the post-medieval phases of cultivation in the glen, rather than being a contemporary response to broken, steep ground.

The most clearly-defined group of terraces lies on the face of the Ochil escarpment above Lipney. The terraces are discrete from one another, exploiting the flatter ground on an otherwise rocky and broken hillside. They vary from 9m to 16m in breadth and from 16m to 70m in length. In some cases rickles of cleared stones extend along the leading scarp of the terrace, and rabbit burrows reveal a deep and well-developed soil to the rear. To the west the extent of available cultivable ground increases and larger plots are defined by spreads of field-gathered stones. This ground has no trace of any rig on it and these plots may also be relics of earlier cultivation. Some

Fig.49 The terraces (A) visible on this vertical aerial photograph (106G/SCOT/UK120 20 June 1946, 3046) on the Ochil escarpment above Foreside of Lipney (Dumyat) probably represent a relatively early period of cultivation. SC 579471

of the terraces elsewhere in the glen, for example on the north bank of the First Inchna Burn, extend for distances over 110m in length.

Head-dykes

While natural features such as watercourses were used as major boundaries between farms, head-dykes divided the common grazings on the hills from the pasture and arable lower down the slope; this division was not hard and fast, and there are a few instances of plots of arable above the dykes (p.20, fig.14; p.47, fig.41). The dykes are generally substantial turf banks, which in some cases still stand up to 1.5m in height. The majority are drawn across the spines of spurs between the precipitous gorges, thus blocking the easier line of access between the watershed and the bottom of the glen. In the upper reaches of the glen the lack of strong topographic features has required the construction of a much more extensive head-dyke to create an effective enclosure.

Phasing in the construction of the dykes is apparent throughout the glen, and generally takes the form of the incorporation of intakes, but can also be seen in the remodelling of an existing boundary (e.g. p.46). We have already seen on the southern flank of Loss Hill (pp.48-9, fig.43), a clear example where the area bounded by a head-dyke has been altered in two distinct stages. There, the denuded turf-dyke that divides the higher portion of the hill is demonstrably earlier than the series of head-dykes that bound the cultivation to the north of Loss farmsteading and the fields above Ashentrool (p.18, fig.11). The surviving portion of this earlier enclosure takes in only grazing, in contrast to the later head-dykes above Loss, which enclose predominantly cultivated ground, albeit along three slightly different alignments. These two major phases of enclosure were evidently predicated on different principles. The existence of the earlier boundary along such a radically different line may well indicate a different pattern of tenure, suggesting that one large unit was subsequently subdivided into at least two separate holdings.

Elsewhere in the glen, the area enclosed by head-dykes appears to have expanded progressively, as indeed has happened with the three dykes forming the second stage of the enclosures above Loss. In these other cases, the pattern

Fig.50 While many of the farms are bounded by natural features, such as can be seen on this vertical aerial photograph (F21.540/RAF/1525 4 February 1955, 0428) of the spur occupied by Inchney, head-dykes were employed to separate the higher pastures from the mosaic of pasture and arable on the middle slopes. The head-dyke (A) above Inchney (B), which has been extended in a secondary stage of construction, can be seen towards the top of the picture, cutting across between the burns. SC 579484

of expansion is revealed by the junction of the various dykes, in which the later ones abut or override an earlier line, e.g. along the north bank of the Third Inchna Burn (p.18, fig.11) and along the south bank of the Second Inchna Burn. In other cases the sequence between head-dykes can only be inferred, such as with the two head-dykes separated by about 300m on the spur above Little Jerah (pp.50-1, fig.45). Here, the outer head-dyke is the better-preserved, and on this basis it has been suggested that it is the later, roughly extending the line of the head-dykes to the north and south of the Inchna Burns. An expansion in the ground enclosed by head-dykes is a recurrent theme in the glen and it may be that some of the phases of enclosure are broadly contemporary.

The dating evidence for the head-dykes in the glen is poor, but the documentary sources show that they were functioning as boundaries in the first half of the 18th century. In 1715, for instance, the incoming tenant of Tounhead of Loss had grazing 'within the dykes and no further';[143] this presumably refers to a head-dyke, although, as we have seen at Lipney, some of the head-dykes incorporate earlier enclosures. Also, in 1732, when a joint tenancy of Lipney was divided between Foreside and Backside,[144] the hill above the highway and the head-dyke was to be held in common. This form of arrangement was maintained in a tack of 1740 for Foreside and Quarterside of Lipney,[145] which stipulated that the common pasturage was to be 'Above the old head dyke' (see also p.23). There is no indication of how old the dyke may have been, but this phrasing need not imply that it was redundant at the time. Nevertheless, the head-dykes are unlikely to have been maintained after the reorganisation of the landscape in the 1760s and the subsequent construction of new march-dykes between the various estates in the glen (pp.58-9). The antiquity of the first use of the head-dykes is less easy to establish. They are certainly not the earliest surviving agricultural features in the glen, and the stimulus for their construction may lie in the pressures generated by the expansion of settlement during the 16th and 17th centuries. Unfortunately, the complex sequences of dykes on some of the spurs, notably on the hill above Loss, need not carry any implications for the age of any of the other boundaries. They may have remained in use for several centuries but, equally, such boundaries could be built fairly quickly, and they may represent relatively short phases of land-use.

Enclosures and fencing
Within the head-dykes there are extensive networks of banks forming enclosures, most of which are 1ha to 2ha in area. The pattern of enclosures suggests a process of accretion, rather than design, and the banks often abut the head-dykes. The flexible management of arable and grazing within the head-dykes, demonstrated by the documentary sources, suggests that many of these enclosures were primarily built for tathing, in which stock were folded on land that was to be cultivated the following season. The repeated overprinting of rig by enclosures, overlain by or interspersed with further cultivation, is a consistent phenomenon in the glen, supporting the documentary evidence that tathing was a major element in the organisation of land-use during the 18th century. Above Ashentrool, for example (p.23, fig.16), the chaotic intermixing of enclosures, banks and rig results from the successive overprinting of land-use regimes, and the only clear pattern involves the disruption of large enclosures by rig.

A tack of 1752 for Backside of Lipney allowed the landlord to 'extend the park dykes of Lipnoch two or three yards upon the said ground if he sees fit to remove the old park dykes'.[146] Wright's notes on sowing at Loss make several references to areas of arable taken in and to old, or former, enclosures; for example, in 1758, oats were sown in the Calfward and on 'the piece now taken in west side of ditto up to the old Pomfold',[147] which was presumably enclosed by dykes. Enclosures could also be created above the head-dykes, as specified in a tack of 1740 for Backside and Quarterside of Lipney.[148] The tenant

was allowed to take in 'an acre more at the west end next to Fossachie Muir'; this may correspond to a discrete patch of cultivation bounded by a turf bank on the north flank of Dumyat (fig.14). Enclosures primarily for stock could also be cultivated, although perhaps only on an *ad hoc* basis. The Nolt Fauld on Loss was sown only once, that being with barley in 1756, 'being tathed with sheep this year'.[149]

Wright built several new stockproof boundaries during the 1750s as part of the emparkment of the ground around Loss (pp.25-6). Some of these are of interest for the evidence they provide concerning the design of the boundaries and their construction. In 1757 three dykes were constructed; each was to be 4 or 4½ feet (1.2m - 1.35m) high, with stones 'put in the founds to keep off the water', and they were to be 'faced' with feal.[150] Two of these dykes are readily identified as those running from the Loss Burn to the steading at Loss, and the third stretches from the garden to the Crunie Burn (p.49, fig.43). On 4th July 1758 Wright commissioned a further dyke 'betwixt the Bridge at Loss and around by the head of Milnfald to the glen at Jeray'.[151] The line was marked out by stakes, indicating that this was a new creation, and it can be identified as the large crescentic dyke above the steading at Loss. The specification for this substantial boundary survives in the Wright papers: it was to comprise a ditch six feet (1.8m) broad at the top, three feet (0.9m) at the bottom by three feet deep, and flanked on the uphill side by a bank three feet high. Even today it is an impressive feature, with a stone face on the uphill side (fig.51). Wright estimated the dyke to be 56 falls long (c.313m), and it was completed by three men within 30 days.[152] A few years later, probably in 1762, a ditch and bank extending from the crescentic dyke around Loss to Tounhead was constructed.[153]

In addition to these stockproof boundaries, Wright laid out other enclosures in the glen designed to protect the trees that he is known to have planted in large numbers. These enclosures lay outwith the immediate policies of Loss, and what are probably plantation boundaries can still be seen in several places, often taking in steep slopes and stream gullies. The best example lies along the south bank of the Menstrie Burn between Backside and Quarterside of Lipney (pp.46-7, fig.41). This enclosure is clearly not for stock, as it takes in the steeply-sloping ground dropping down to the burn, though the boundary would have been stockproof. Other enclosures appear to have taken in grazing alone, for example on the east flank of Dumyat, above Quarterside of Lipney (p.47, fig.41). Their interiors show no sign of having been ploughed and, while their function is unclear, they may have been tathed, but never cultivated.

Fencing or palings are mentioned by Wright during the 1750s, and the use of these less durable materials in the new enclosures clearly became more important after 1761, when he took up the lease for Fossachie, to the west of the survey area. Palings were cheap and fast to put up, an important consideration with rented ground.[154] Some insights into the character of the boundaries that Wright was creating in his haste to enclose at this time are provided by a memorandum dated 2nd January 1761:

'*Inclose at Broomhill & stake out ditto ground*
Make stakes for pealing and bespeak firrs
Prepare to lead stones
De Mending slaps in dykes at Cadger knows
Make pealing and hedge up from Carly house up to ye heid
except where ye Burn cross, make that of stone'

Subsequent accounts show that each of these tasks was duly performed.[155] Not only were old dykes being kept up in places, but new boundaries were being constructed from a mixture of materials. The combination of paling and hedge, however, may have been no more than the normal procedure for establishing a hedge, producing a stockproof barrier while the saplings grew up.

Sir   Loss 4 July 1758

I hereby accept of the
offer you make me of the nine pence for
every Six Ells of the Ditch I work to you betwixt
the Bridge at Loss and around by the head of Milnfald
to the glen at Jeray as the Same is marked by Stakes
which Ditch is to be Six foot wide at the Surface three
foot Deep and three foot wide at the bottom and three
foot raised with feall above the surface which feall is to
be eight inches broad   and I hereby promise to doe the
Said Dick & Ditch Sufficient and Compleat the same
betwixt & the twenty fourth day of August next
and in case Im a looser by the bargain I expect you
*4sh will give me Some Shillings * to the bargain and if
Im a gainer by the bargain I shall ask nothing more
than the forsd nine pence for each Six Ells as afrsd

                                    Nicol McAleist
                                              er

To James Wright of Loss

1758   Nicol McKalyster finished part of ye Ditch his Days and
Augt 26   Lads makes in all by my acctt 90 days Supposing them
              7d per day all overhead is £2.12.6

              The number of fals they finished is 56 reckoning them at
              9d as above is   £2 . 2
              and wtin will more ____ . 4
              ~~gave him~~   2 . 6

                     as I found he was a looser
                     by ye bargain I gave him in money   4____
                     all which is pd as below   £2.10s Sterling

                     by Cash at 3
                     Different times   £- 18
                     By 1 B 1f 1p meal at **   17 . 6
                     By cash of this date   14 . 6
                                              £2 .10 . -

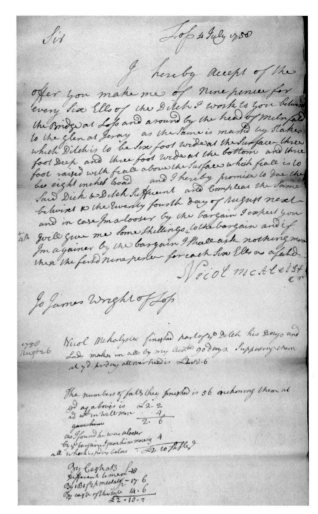

*A   Reproduced by permission of the Keeper of the Records of Scotland
(NAS, RH/15/115/3/1, Bundle K).*

B

Fig.51A-B   The remains of the dyke commissioned from Nicol McAleister (A), and built in July and August 1758, can be seen in this ground view (B), which looks south-east down towards the steading at Loss in the middle of the picture. The stone outer face of the dyke, which is fronted by a ditch, is plainly visible. SC 579435

The use of fencing for internal divisions became increasingly common during the second half of the 18th and the 19th centuries. By 1764, Wright's enclosures at Broomhill comprised 56 falls (313m) of stone dykes and 93 falls (520m) of palings, and later tacks refer to other palings or fences. In 1782, the tack of Loss and Lipney allowed the tenant to cut blackthorn and hazel to make palings,[156] and the tack of 1808 for Fossachie mentions that £192 had already been spent on fencing,[157] probably a reference to the iron post-and-wire fences on the western slopes of Dumyat.

Small enclosures

Most of the documentary evidence for enclosure refers to what were either fields or land divisions. The archaeological survey, however, has also revealed a range of small enclosures that are, for the most part, undocumented. These range widely in size but generally measure less than 40m square. As a group they must have fulfilled a variety of functions, from folding stock to storing winter fodder, but there are few clues as to how individual examples were used. They tend to be located on rough ground beyond the edges of cultivated ground, and so probably relate to grazing practices. Some may have fulfilled similar roles to the three stone-walled sheepfolds in the glen (p.28, fig.21), two of which (Jerah and Second Inchna Burn) are shown on the OS 6-inch map of 1865-6.[158]

Of the smaller enclosures, four may be sheep buchts, one situated above Jerah, the second on the western flank of Colsnaur Hill, the third at Little Jerah (p.51, fig.45), and the fourth along the Third Inchna Burn. This type of long, narrow, subrectangular enclosure, with an entrance in one end, has been recorded widely in the Southern Uplands, where they occur in large numbers. There it is suggested they were primarily for milking sheep, although they may have been used also for other activities, such as shearing.[159] On Colsnaur Hill and Little Jerah, the buchts abut the head-dykes, but otherwise there is no direct evidence for their dating. They were evidently not common in the Ochils, and only two examples were discovered during the survey of an adjacent area in Glen Devon.

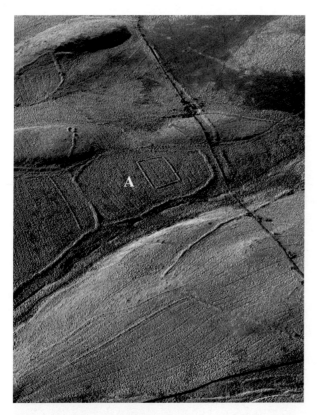

Fig.52 Some of the small enclosures that have been recorded overlie cultivation remains, as can be seen in this oblique aerial view from the west of an example (A) north of Ashentrool. SC 611363

Marches

The majority of stone march-dykes separating the major properties in the glen were largely constructed in the 1760s; before then few of the boundaries appear to have been set out with artificial markers. The boundaries of the medieval properties, for instance, can only be defined loosely today (p.16), although some, such as those of Jerah, made use of the deeply incised burns. Elsewhere, other less well-defined topographical features may have formed the marches. In these cases the march was liable to dispute, as happened at Fossachie, where the boundaries were the subject of arbitration in 1590, though the details of the dispute are obscure.[160] The complexity of the holdings before the improvements has already been described (p.16), citing the case of Lossintrule in the early 18th century, where lands were still held in runrig and the tenants of more than one laird had access to the same common grazings.[161] Even when Lossintrule was divided between Stirling of Keir and Wright of Loss in 1754, the respective holdings remained interspersed and there was no march-dyke.[162] However, during the early 18th century there are signs that the definitions of marches were becoming of more significance. A tack of 1732 for Parsonleys, a property to the north-west of the glen (p.19, fig.12), defined its bounds.[163] The background to this need for clarifying the bounds is revealed in the Wright papers; Linton of Pendreich, who owned Parsonleys, complained angrily that James Wright (snr) had not merely connived at, but had assisted with, the demolition of a march-dyke recently put up to protect his tenant's grass.[164]

Such disputes were inevitable in the absence of fixed boundaries, but the interspersed character of the holdings on properties such as Lossintrule was also liable to frustrate the improving ambitions of landlords. It is not surprising, therefore, that the 1760s saw a process of rationalisation of the properties and their boundaries. Indeed, most of the march-dykes that are now such a prominent feature of the glen were laid out in the early 1760s and the progress of their construction can be traced in the documentation. The division of Lossintrule in 1754 had evidently not produced a long-lasting solution, for on 10th January 1761 Stirling of Keir wrote to Wright agreeing to a new division. Wright was in a hurry to finalise the agreement, perhaps to protect his investment in the Loss mine (pp.60-1) and at first agreed to almost any terms, only later refining his position.[165] The Contract of Division and Excambion is dated 6th April 1762.[166] It noted that the previous division had left the high ground undivided, that parts of the march were irregular and still 'contraverted', and that the farms of Longcraig, Whittetsbank, Ploverburn, Cauldhame and Callander were scattered and interspersed with one another. The new division was intended to be not only equal, but also regular. The line of the new march was described in detail:

'From the east gavel of the sheep house of Ashentrool …in a direct straight line north by the Peat Road crossing the Stripe to a Pitt and March Stones fixed therein in the Boig at the back and on the East side of the field of Ashentrool called Broadleys, And from thence east by another straight line through the ground formerly contraverted and the Balloch hill formerly a commonty to the March in the slack at Balloch …terminating about two hundred and forty yards above the Brown Hill'

This clearly corresponds to the line of the march-dyke that extends north from the Lossburn reservoir onto Loss Hill and across to the gully called The Balloch on the east of Brown Hill (fig.53). The division of Longcraig, Whittetsbank, Ploverburn, Callander and Cauldhame was also to be defined by a new march, beginning:

Fig.53 *The march-dyke between Loss and Ashentrool, seen here in this ground view looking northwards to the west flank of Loss Hill, was laid out in 1762. The green rise in the level of the ground in the centre of the picture marks the site of Patrick Henderson's sheep-house, which is mentioned in the description of the march contained in James Wright's papers. SC 585622*

'*At the pit and march stone on the grounds of Callander at the march with Pendreich. And from that goes in a straight line through the Croft of Callander to a Sauchin Gushet between the west end of the two Southmost ridges of the lands of Cauldhame, from thence in another straight line northeast through the Callander Lone to another Pitt and March Stones placed near to the North west corner of that part of the lands of Cauldhame called Ewan's Fold to another Pitt and stones placed at the Head dyke and from that in a straight line through the commonty belonging to the said lands to the March between it and the Park of Jeray*'

Further memoranda and accounts record the progress of the new march-dykes built in the glen between 1763 and 1765, including a ditch at Backside of Lipney, involving around 150 man-days work.[167] Hedging was clearly as useful for defining the marches as it was for lesser boundaries. In 1764, 5,000 thorns were delivered to Loss, and 2,000 of them were planted on the march between Fossachie and Ashentrool along the Loss Burn, in the area now largely drowned by the reservoir. In 1765 a further 10,500 thorns were planted in a double row on the same march after it had been straightened by a surveyor.[168]

The drystone walls that subdivide the north-west sector of the glen were also built at this time. Fossachie was to be enclosed with a stone dyke following an agreement in 1760, a considerable expense to the landlord, Haldane, for which Wright had to pay 7% interest.[169] In 1768, a new dyke was built between Keir's lands of Ashentrool and Wright's lands of Lipney, running along the Loss Burn to the west of the Kirk Ford.[170]

This burst of activity was not confined to Menstrie Glen. To the east, Balquharn Glen was turned over to sheep by 1759 and when it was subdivided in 1768 a new march was defined.[171] In 1761, Wright proposed to the proprietors of Drumdruills and Pendreich, to the west of the glen, that the Auld Wharry Burn should be straightened and adopted as a march.[172]

Once laid out, the marches were rapidly established as the major divisions of the landscape. Not all were to survive in use, however, and the amalgamation of properties in the 19th century made some of them redundant. In these cases, the dykes were often left to fall into disrepair, but this could also be the fate of the marches that were retained. In 1813, for example, '*much of the fence*' between Loss and Jerah was defective.[173]

Sheep-houses

Not all the buildings that have been mapped in the course of the archaeological survey were intended for human habitation, and it can be shown that at least two were constructed to provide roofed shelter for sheep at night. Known as sheep-houses, most of the recorded examples in Scotland are of 19th-century date,[174] but documentary sources refer to them from the late 17th century onwards.[175] In Menstrie Glen the records of sheep-houses date from the mid-18th century. These refer to the use and maintenance of at least five and, in two cases, at Ashentrool and on the hillside north of Loss, detailed descriptions have allowed their remains to be identified.

The sheep-house at Ashentrool can be identified from the description of the new march constructed following the division of Lossintrule. This ran '*from the east gavel of the sheep house at Ashentrool possessed by Patrick Henderson*',[176] and the footings of only one building match this description. Apart from being one of the largest buildings in the glen, measuring 12.2m by 3.1m internally and with three compartments, it is an unremarkable structure. The second sheep-house is described in documents about Loss dated 1744 and 1745 that refer to the repair of the *'sheep house up the hill'*.[177] This structure lies on the south flank of Loss Hill (p.49, fig.43), and is equally unremarkable in its form. It is slightly smaller than that at Ashentrool, measuring 10m by 3.5m transversely within faced-rubble footings 0.7m in thickness, and has an entrance in the centre of one side. The documents record its repair and imply that it was a thatched structure. Dung was taken from the sheep-house to be spread on the arable fields. An idea scrawled by Wright on a scrap of paper suggests *'when putting sheep into a house at night take a candle before them'*,[178] a proposition that may not often have been practical.

The other sheep-houses referred to in the mid-18th century were at Foreside of Lipney, where there were two,[179] and at Backside of Lipney.[180] There was also another sheep-house close to, or forming part of the steading at Loss; this may be the same sheep-house for which payment was made for nine half days work *'quarrying stones'* in 1753.[181]

The examples that have been identified at Ashentrool and Loss, however, are essentially indistinguishable from the remains of many other buildings with stone footings that survive in the glen. Indeed, it is probably for this reason alone that the sheep-house at Backside of Lipney, for which there is no contemporary description of its location, has not been identified on the ground. The same may be true at Foreside, although here the sheep-house may have been obliterated by later activity. Other examples may well lie undetected among the buildings recorded in the course of the archaeological survey elsewhere, particularly on the east side of the glen or amongst some of the larger buildings recorded at several shieling sites (p.30). The presence of at least five such buildings on the west side of Menstrie Glen in the 18th century makes it clear that these buildings were a recurrent element of pre-improvement farms in the area.

Mining

During the 18th and 19th centuries the landlords of many estates were well aware of the wealth that could be accrued from mineral deposits that lay on their lands. Accordingly, they often invested in at least limited searches for minerals, and many upland areas bear the scars of such trials. Menstrie Glen is no exception, the physical evidence of mineral exploitation of this date comprising the appositely named Loss Copper Mine, situated about 1km north-west of Loss, and numerous small-scale trials, both there and on Lipney (fig.54). Subsequently, probably during the 19th century, a calcite mine was opened on Myreton Hill on the east side of the glen. There is a tradition that heavy metal mining in the Ochils dates from the medieval period, but no documentary sources have been found to confirm this. It is not until 1696 that documentation refers to local mines, in this case probably somewhere near Blairlogie. A contract for work stipulated that the *'old mine'* was to be drained and, while there is no indication of the date of these earlier workings, they are securely in the 17th century.[182] The large quantity of silver produced by the Alva mines in 1714-15 would also undoubtedly have stimulated the interest of men like James Wright in the mineral wealth of the Ochils. In general, however, this interest was not repaid, and acrimony and financial loss were evidently the keynotes of most of the 18th-century ventures. This was certainly the case in Menstrie Glen.

The main focus of the copper mining was a seam that had been discovered on Loss Hill (fig.55). A single adit was driven into the west flank of the hill, and a scatter of trials were sunk around the southern slopes (p.49, fig.43). The rock-cut entrance to the adit lies at the back of a terrace, and its line to the south-east is marked by a row of hollows where the roof

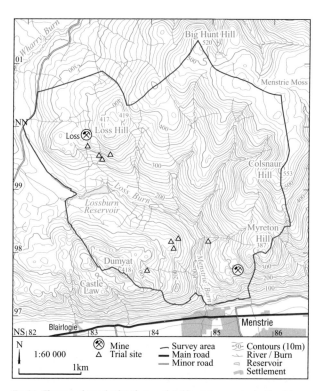

Fig.54 *This map shows the distribution of visible mining remains in Menstrie Glen. With the exception of the Calcite mine above Menstrie, most of the mining activity probably dates from the 18th century and was associated with the extraction of copper from a seam discovered on Loss Hill.*

Fig.55 *The entrance to the Loss Copper Mine is still open. SC 579458*

has collapsed into the passage below. There was presumably a crushing floor outside the mine, probably on the adjacent spoil heap, but no trace of it can be detected.

The other workings in the vicinity appear to be on a smaller scale, and for this reason have been interpreted as trials. To the south of the adit a trench no more than 2m in length is visible, while further round the slope to the south-east, immediately above the old head-dyke, there is a cluster of shallow pits and trenches with adjacent piles of spoil. Workings across the rest of the glen are equally small-scale, comprising small pits and narrow trenches up to 10m in length. Most of these are concentrated on the eastern flank of Dumyat (see p.47, fig.41), but a single example lies on the south bank of the First Inchna Burn. It is conceivable that other trials in the areas below the head-dykes have been obscured by subsequent cultivation (below).

The complex and protracted business background to these rather insignificant remains is illuminated by the Wright of Loss papers and other documentation. The earliest record of mining in the glen dates to 1722, and by 1726, over 120 stones of ore had been removed from the mine at Loss for analysis.[183] Further work undertaken in 1727 and 1729 may not have been entirely to the liking of James Wright's grandfather, who claimed in a note preserved amongst the Wright papers that the miners had damaged 12 falls of ground in the immediate vicinity of their working, a further 12 falls of arable ground, and 24 falls of pasture.[184] This venture clearly fizzled out, and in May 1735 four iron mells, four picks, eight jumpers, one womb and six wedges were removed from Tounhead of Loss, *'belonging to the company of miners that wrought there'*.[185] Correspondence in November 1753 deals with *'cleaning out the mouth of the drift and getting fore-end driven'*, but this work seems to have come to nothing.[186] Similarly, in June 1758 a Mr Willson wrote to Wright, reminding him that the results of his prospection had revealed several very promising sites, and urging Wright to exploit the minerals he had found. Willson was seeking some reward for his expertise, but again nothing was done.

This phase of activity does not seem to have been marked by any great success, although in 1761 James Wright claimed that six tons of ore had been removed in his grandfather's time.[187] However, Wright had been trying to attract new business partners to develop the mines in the 1750s and 1760s, and he had every reason to put a favourable gloss on the results of the earlier venture.

In 1760 Wright entered into a contract with a Mr Weston of Lambeth to undertake further mining work.[188] Ground was evidently broken but, in January and April 1761, Wright wrote angrily to Weston, demanding compensation; the work had lapsed and he claimed that he had missed other opportunities for exploiting the mines.[189] In July, Wright made a formal protest and broke the contract with Weston.[190] In the meantime, he was already in negotiation with James Stephens to obtain a contract with an English partnership involved with several other local mines.[191] Contracts seem to have been exchanged early in 1762 and some work was undertaken,[192] but there had been no progress by December.[193] Drainage of water in the workings may have been a problem at Loss, but in 1763 hopes that the venture might still come good were being expressed.[194] This must have been a forlorn hope and, although Wright's break with this partnership is not documented, the Loss mine seems to have been abandoned shortly afterwards. The story of the Loss mine appears to have been typical of the attempts to exploit the minerals of the area, which consistently failed to fulfil the promise offered by the Alva mines at the beginning of the 18th century.

Little is known of the other mining enterprise in Menstrie Glen, namely the small-scale calcite mine on the south face of Myreton Hill (fig.56). Calcite is a crystalline form of calcium carbonate and, to judge by the size of the workings, the seam here appears to have varied between 2.7m and 4.2m in thickness. The date of the mine is uncertain, and it is not known what the calcite was being used for, although it has been considered too impure for chemical purposes.[195] The mine comprises four discrete quarries, each with an adjacent mound of spoil. A graded pony track zigzags up the face of the escarpment to link three of the workings.

Fig.56 This ground view looks into one of the four quarries of the calcite mine on Myreton Hill.
SC 579488

CONCLUSIONS

The stimulus for the archaeological survey of Menstrie Glen was initially provided by a perceived threat to archaeological remains in the Ochils posed by forestry developments. In this sense, the survey was little different to those carried out by the Royal Commission in other parts of Scotland, where equivalent landscapes have also been preserved by the contraction of settlement and arable agriculture over the last 150-250 years. In its execution, however, this project changed its character, almost entirely due to the quality of the surviving manuscript sources relating to the glen. These have turned the project from a routine exercise in the recovery and recording of archaeological remains in the landscape, to an opportunity to get to grips with the ways in which this landscape has been exploited over the last 500 years. This is a sweeping claim, particularly in view of the paucity of the earlier historical records, but one that can be justified on the range and detail of the information contained within the Wright of Loss papers. Most of this relates to the 18th century, and, crucially, to the period from 1750 to 1769, when Wright was managing the estate himself and embarked upon the radical changes that transformed the landscape in the glen. Wright has bequeathed us a documentary landscape, coloured with his observations, and populated with his tenants and workers, while the glen itself presents us with a well-preserved archaeological landscape. From these two strands of evidence has emerged a picture of settlement and land-use that has rarely been glimpsed in Scotland, giving a rare insight into the workings of the farming landscape both before and at the time of the Improvements.

Of particular note in the Menstrie Glen material is the illustration of the rapid transformation of rural Scotland during the mid- to late 18th century, driven in part by a desire for increased production and profit, but also by a broad ideological mission to improve society.[196] To a limited extent Wright was in the vanguard of the Improving movement. He corresponded with Lord Kames, one of the prime movers in feeding the Scottish Enlightenment into the agricultural sphere,[197] and is a rare example of an owner directly involved in the improvement of his own small estate.

Despite the remarkable combination of historical and archaeological sources that has been achieved during the project, we should not lose sight of the original objectives

of the archaeological survey, namely the assessment of the archaeological potential of the Ochils. In numerical terms, the results of the survey speak for themselves. Where there were previously seven archaeological records, there are now no fewer than 87 (p.14). In nearby Glen Devon, surveyed in 1998, the equivalent figures are about 20 and 90. As in Menstrie Glen, the preponderance of the sites and monuments identified date from the last 500 years or so, although the pattern of dykes, enclosures and rig that was mapped evidently reveal slightly different patterns of land-use (below). It is reasonable to suppose that a comparable enhancement in the numbers of entries held in local Sites and Monuments Records and the NMRS would be achieved by survey throughout the Ochils. That said, the emphasis of the archaeological remains surviving in this landscape lies firmly with their use in the post-medieval period. That much is evident from the extent of relict cultivation remains, field-systems and enclosures that have been mapped from vertical aerial photographs taken shortly after World War II (fig.57). These reveal huge swathes of ground beyond the modern fields that were enclosed and cultivated prior to the Improvements. As a result of this intense later land-use, prehistoric monuments are relatively few and far between. The presence of a dun at the mouth of Menstrie Glen, therefore, is of considerable significance, as is a cairn and ditched barrow that came to light in the course of the work in Glen Devon. The scatter of such monuments suggests that this range of hills was exploited throughout prehistory, and that the general absence of settlements dating from before the medieval period is a question of their visibility and survival in the face of extensive and intensive later land-use.

In Menstrie Glen itself, it is evident that the intensity of land-use reaches a peak in the first half of the 18th century. This has severely curtailed the opportunity to discover visible settlement remains dating from before 1700, other than the shieling-huts upon the higher pastures. Nevertheless, the possibility that some of the turf-walled byre-houses represent elements in an earlier pattern of settlement, perhaps dating from the late 17th century, is raised by their locations beyond the head-dykes (p.33). If it were possible to demonstrate that the head-dykes were amongst the earliest components in this landscape, this argument might carry greater weight. As we have seen, however, they are not (pp.46 and 56), and may only

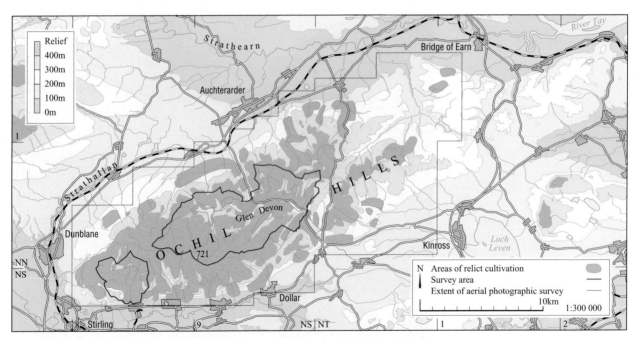

Fig.57 Comparable landscapes to that recorded in Menstrie Glen are found widely throughout the Ochil Hills. This map depicts the rough extent of relict cultivation systems recorded on vertical aerial photographic sources held in the NMRS, supplemented by ground survey in Menstrie Glen and Glen Devon.

Fig.58 This ground view looks out of the glen towards the west-south-west, across Foreside of Lipney (now Dumyat Farm) to the Wallace Monument. The archaeological remains within Menstrie Glen are probably a manifestation of practices that were employed widely in the neighbouring lowlands but, there, the banks and rigs have long since been ploughed away. SC 579467

come into existence when the landscape was already densely occupied. This does not preclude any of these byre-houses dating from the late 17th century, but the evidence from Cadger Knowes points to the existence of a raft of minor settlements that must have housed the poorest tenants or cottars in the first half of the 18th century. These settlements would almost certainly occupy the less attractive locations, which is precisely where they have turned up along the northern flank of Dumyat.

The complexity of the land-use remains in Menstrie Glen is typical of the uplands throughout eastern Scotland and the Borders. Enclosures containing traces of cultivation rigs, defined by turf banks that have been remodelled successively on numerous occasions, have been recorded by other Royal Commission surveys,[198] and they figure extensively in the collection of aerial photographs held by the NMRS. The detail contained within the Wright papers has provided an insight into the practices that were involved in the construction and cultivation of these enclosures that has otherwise proved elusive. These are almost certainly the temporary folds erected in the course of tathing. This practice of folding stock onto areas that were intended to be under arable in the following year also underpinned the intermittent cultivation on some of the better pastures. It explains the chaotic character of the remains of some of these enclosures, which on the ground can rarely be resolved stratigraphically into discrete fields or systems. It is clear from the remains in Menstrie Glen, however, that in places the areas covered by the blocks of rigs entirely subsume ground that was formerly enclosed by turf-banked enclosures. This may be a manifestation of the expansion of arable ground documented in the first half of the 18th century (p.21), as regular cultivation took in ground that was previously only intermittently tathed.

The character of the later land-use in the rest of the Ochils is to some extent illustrated by the picture that has emerged from Menstrie Glen. The transfer of land to local lairds during

the late-15th and 16th centuries, the establishment of a dense pattern of tenanted farms by the 17th century, the dramatic contraction of settlement after the mid-18th century, and the creation of sheep walks, are general themes that recur across wide areas of Scotland. The survey of Glen Devon, however, shows that there can be considerable variation in the detail of settlement and land-use over relatively short distances. In Glen Devon, for instance, there are large areas of enclosed grazing alongside the cultivated ground. This complements the predominance of stock in the economy that emerges from the documentary sources for Glen Devon. Livestock were of particular importance there through the 17th and 18th centuries, and the pressures on grazings appear to have been significant from as early as the 16th century. Many of the farms in Glen Devon were large and well capitalised by the late 16th century, and a clutch of substantial farm houses dating from the 17th and early 18th century are testament to the wealth generated from livestock by a handful of families during this period. From the 1760s, however, there was a new phase of re-capitalisation and re-organisation, dominated by in-comers, James Wright of Loss among them. Indeed, it is the Wright of Loss papers that illuminate the pattern of 18th-century management in Glen Devon.

Despite the contrasts in some of the detail between the two areas, there can be little doubt that the pre-Improvement farming landscape that had emerged in Menstrie Glen by the 18th century would have been familiar across wide areas of eastern Scotland. In this respect, the archaeological remains in Menstrie Glen are not simply relicts of a failed agriculture system in the uplands. They are a manifestation of social and economic processes that were also in operation in the Lowlands, where the archaeological evidence is now largely removed (fig.58). Thus, Wright's papers and the landscape of Menstrie Glen contain a national dimension that is of interest to historians and archaeologists alike.

JAMES WRIGHT OF LOSS: 1730-69

Much of the wealth of documentation relating to Menstrie Glen was generated or collected by James Wright, laird of Loss during the middle decades of the 18th century. In addition to the insights that his near-obsessive notes have already provided into the management of his estate and business, they also throw light on the man himself and his family life.

James Wright (Wright hereafter) was a minor when he inherited Loss in 1745 following the death of his father (also James).[199] The Wrights had been portioners of Loss since shortly before 1680, and Wright also inherited Lipney and an interest in Freuchie in Fife.[200] In the late 1740s he was studying in Edinburgh but, after considering other careers,[201] he returned to Dunblane about 1750. Among his Dunblane neighbours were the Drummonds (alias MacGregor) of Balhaldie, with whom Prince Charles Edward Stewart had stayed in 1746. One of the Drummond daughters, loyally named Jacobina, wrote to Wright on 12th June 1749 (fig.60), thanking him for some books, and reporting that there was no news; the letter coyly ends '*PS I shall be glad to hear from you as often as it is agreeable and convenient*'.[202] Wright treasured the note and married the writer, gaining many impecunious relatives into the bargain. They had a daughter, Margaret ('Peggy'), but she died on 2nd September 1752.[203] In spring 1753 the Wrights moved to the extensively renovated mansion house of Loss. By this time Wright was farming Loss on his own account, and administering the rest of his own estate as well as that of Balhaldie. He was obviously very successful with these and other ventures (see below), and by 1764 he was able to purchase Argyll's Lodging in Stirling, one of the most magnificent town houses in Scotland, which he extensively renovated (fig.59).[204] In late 1769 he died of 'apoplexy' after a short illness, and was buried in the former Earl of Stirling's aisle at Holy Rude Kirk, Stirling. The majority of his estate passed to his cousin, also James Wright, the minister of Logie, although an attempt to make Jacobina's nephew his heir a few days before his death seems to have caused considerable confusion.[205]

Wright's business interests were astonishingly varied and extensive. For several years he employed Alpine Drummond as a drover, purchasing beasts in the Highlands and elsewhere for resale; the success of this business is indicated by Drummond's wages, rising from £24 a year in 1756-7 to £48 in 1760.[206] From time to time he bought and sold grain and other commodities,[207] and he seems to have had a short-term interest in some of the Clackmannanshire coal mines.[208] He does not appear to have acted on proposals that he should invest in a West Indian plantation – complete with slaves.[209] Wright also travelled extensively, visiting the Uists in 1763 and London and Paris in 1764. On the trip to the Uists he carried with him a recommendation to the gentlemen of the Uists, and perhaps it was for that trip that he also had a note of some polite phrases in Gaelic.[210] During his absences he kept in regular touch with Jacobina, who took over management of the farms, and she would inform him of the jobs in hand. For example, she wrote '*the Fossachie sheep were sorted on Monday ... and only about 25 are good*' and went on to tell him that she had not sent any to market as she could not make up a sufficient flock.[211] On another occasion she told him '*the grass at Back of Dykes was stoud as I expected you was to keep it for hay. It looks very well and is well kept but if you order it to be ate it will soon make the sheep good*'.[212]

The Wrights were in intermittent touch with various of Jacobina's emigrant relatives. One of them, Donald Drummond, assured them that '*there is hardly an honest man*

Fig.59   Argyll's Lodging, Stirling, one of the grandest town houses in Scotland, was purchased by James Wright in 1764. SC 498055

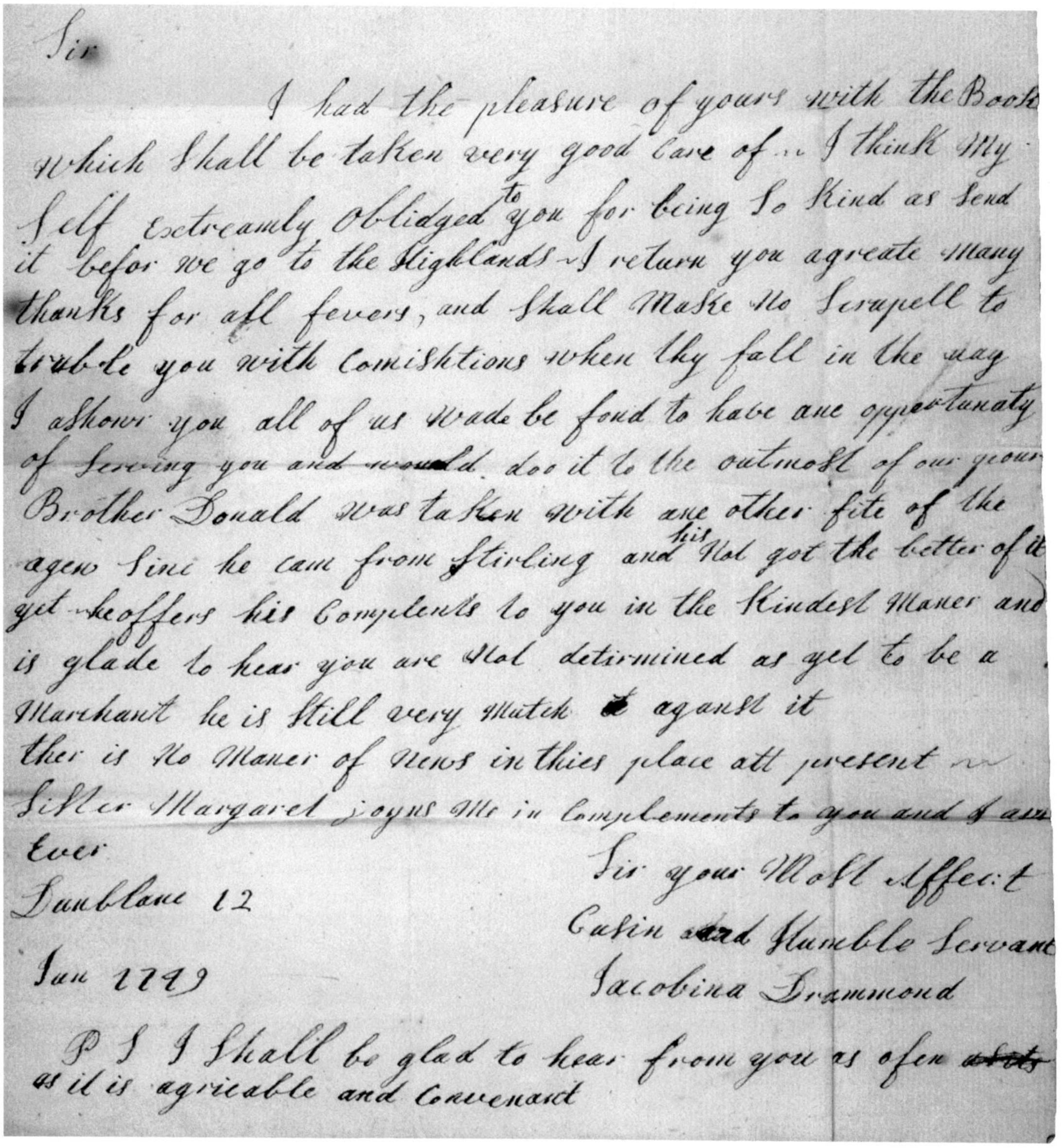

Sir

I had the pleasure of yours with the Book which Shall be taken very good Care of... I think My Self Extreamly Oblidged to you for being So Kind as Send it befor we go to the Highlands ~ I return you agreate many thanks for all fevers, and Shall Make No Scrupell to truble you with Comishtions when thy fall in the way I ashowr you all of us wade be fond to have ane opportunaty of Serving you ~~and would~~ doo it to the outmost of our powr Brother Donald was taken with ane other fite of the agew Sine he cam from Stirling and his Not got the better of it yet he offers his Complents to you in the Kindest Maner and is glade to hear you are Not detirmined as yet to be a Marchant he is Still very Match agansit it ther is No Maner of News in thies place att present ~ Sister Margaret joyns Me in Complements to you and I am Ever

Dunblane 12
Jun 1749

Sir your Most Affec:t
Cusin and Humble Servant
Jacobina Drummond

P S I Shall be glad to hear from you as ofen ~~as its~~ as it is agrieable and Convenant

Sir

I had the pleasure of yours with the Book
which shall be taken very good care of. I think my
self extreamly oblidged [to] *you for being so kind as send*
it befor we go to the Highlands ~ I return you a greate many
thanks for all fevers (favours)*, and shall make no scrupell to*
truble you with comishtions (commissions) *when they fall in the way*
I ashowr (assure) *you all of us wade be fond to have ane opportunaty*
of serving you and would doe it to the outmost of our powr
Brother Donald was taken with ane other fite of the
ageu since he came from Stirling and [his] *not got the better of it*
yet he offers his complemts to you in the kindest manner and
is glade to hear you are not detirmined as yet to be a
marchant he is still very match aganst it
ther is no maner of news in thies place att present ~
Sister Margaret joyns me in complements to you and I am

Ever	*Sir your most Affec:t*
Dunblane 12	*Cusin and Humble servant*
Jun 1749	*Jacobina Drummond*

P S I shall be glad to hear from you as ofen ~~as its~~
as it is agrieable and convenant

Fig.60 This letter, dated 12 June 1749, was written by Jacobina Drummond to James Wright at the beginning of their courtship. Reproduced by permission of the Keeper of the Records of Scotland (NAS, RH15/115/4/1, Bundle D).

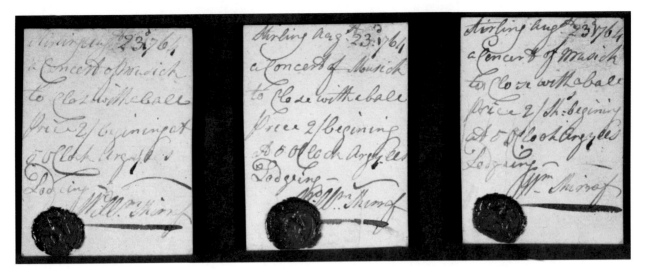

Fig.61 These tickets were for a 'concert of musick to close with a ball' at Argyll's Lodging in August 1764. Reproduced by permission of the Keeper of the Records of Scotland (NAS, RH15/115/3/2, Bundle D).

in all North America'.[213] Having married into an impecunious family, requests for money were frequent. An L. Drummond was the most persistent correspondent: Wright was '*the only friend I have on earth*'[214]; again and again, he needed just £5, and it would always be the last time. Others contacted him for help to get a job, a lease, a promotion, or to get them out of some kind of trouble.[215]

Wright put much effort into his wide range of personal contacts. He made frequent memoranda of 'good ideas', some gleaned on his travels or from visitors,[216] others from suggestions that came by letter (fig.62). In 1763, for example, James McAdam wrote, advising him on management of his Glen Devon flocks and discussing other contemporary farming issues.[217] Wright must have read books on agriculture – indeed, one of his correspondents was Lord Kames of the Blair Drummond Estate [218]– and he certainly bought and probably borrowed books on a wide range of topics. The Wrights corresponded regularly with local gentry, and also with a few from further afield. There are affable invitations from the Bruces of Kennet, the adieus of Abercrombie of Tulllibody before going off on a journey, and a request from Mrs Haldane of Gleneagles to borrow one of the Fossachie milk goats for the sake of her health.[219] Sadly, whilst we have a great many letters to the Wrights, we have few by them – although sometimes a subject was important enough for Wright to keep a draft of his own letter. A letter by Mr Auld, suggesting that the circuit judges might rent Argyll's Lodging, shows just how useful extensive contacts and good humour could be. The judges used to pay six guineas each time, reported Auld, but nine or even ten guineas might not be grudged, '*but that between ourselves*'.[220] The Wrights' central role in local society is also indicated by the great ball which they hosted at Argyll's Lodging in 1764 (fig.61).[221]

Wright's correspondents include the Jacobite Oliphants of Gask (relatives by marriage) and several of his contacts are jocularly 'Jacobitical'. He was personally informed of the death of Cameron of Lochiel, whose genealogy he had researched,[222] and news of the Appin Murder reached Loss within a few days.[223] However, it is improbable that he took Jacobitism very seriously. He was the business partner of the Lord Justice Clerk, rented Argyll's Lodging to the Justiciary Circuit Court judges, became a JP, sat as a juror, was on the Commission for Logie Roads, and spent years on an eventually successful campaign to have his cousin (and eventual heir) appointed Minister for Logie. Nevertheless, his 1760 advertisement for Lipney is the work of an early Romantic: '*the house of Lipney is pleasantly situated upon ye south side of the hill, immediately above the low grounds from whence there is a very fine commanding prospect of a beautyfull country and the River of fforth*'.[224]

The visitors to Loss included a succession of people with health problems to see Jacobina, who had a reputation as a healer, in particular of eyes. Young Archie Campbell's eyes made close study difficult, and he stayed for many months whilst attending school in Dunblane. '*All the redress we wish for is that he may have his sight*', Jacobina wrote.[225] However, there was also a commercial dimension to Jacobina's healing, as can be seen when John Graham of Glengyle asked for some more of the ointment for his daughter's eyes; his post script reads '*Receive a cow*'.[226] Wright's cousin and Edinburgh lawyer, James Fergus, wrote frequent letters full of jocular asides; he, too, loved to visit the '*healthful braes of Loss*'.[227] The goat herds at Lipney and Fossachie were another asset to what almost amounted to an 18th-century health farm.

Wright was a well-known and respected figure. His correspondents were sometimes angry with him (usually for long delays in the payment of debts), but they were more often amiable and trusted him to help them. In addition to the requests for loans, he was repeatedly asked to use his influence (personal, local, national) on someone else's behalf. On several occasions he was asked to undertake the delicate task of arbitrating between disputing neighbours.[228] All in all, he emerges as a genial, worldly-wise man, interested in everything and everyone, a man of his times, a loving husband and a respected neighbour.

Fig.62 A letter addressed to James Wright at Loss, one of many contained within his papers. Reproduced by permission of the Keeper of the Records of Scotland (NAS, RH15/115/5/1, Bundle I).

NOTES

The following abbreviations have been used in the notes:
NAS – *National Archives of Scotland*
GCA – *Glasgow City Archives*
RGS – *Registrar General for Scotland*
SCA – *Stirling Council Archives*
NLS – *National Library of Scotland*
The Census Returns are held by the Registrar General for
Scotland, but they are also available on microfilm.
The Ordnance Survey Name Books are held in the National
Archives of Scotland, but they are also available for public
consultation in the National Monuments Record of Scotland.

PREFACE
1   NAS, RH15/115/3/2, Bundle B, Advertisement of Lipney, 1760. The farm
    is now known as Dumyat.

INTRODUCTION
2   NAS, RH15/115/3/2, Bundle B, Memorandum about Advertisement of
    Lipney, 1760.

SOURCE MATERIAL
3   *The Statistical Account of Scotland*, iii, 1792; *The New Statistical Account*
    of Scotland: Volume VIII, Dumbarton – Stirling – Clackmannan, 1845;
    The Third Statistical Account of Scotland: The counties of Stirling and
    Clackmannan, 1966.
4   Menzies Fergusson, R 1905, *Logie: A Parish History*.
5   Watson, A 1995, *The Ochils: Placenames, History, Tradition*.
6   Roy, W 1747-55, Military Survey of Scotland.
7   NLS, James Stobie 1783, The Counties of Perth and Clackmannan.
8   NLS, S N Morrison 1848, Map of the County of Clackmannan.
9   Harrison, J G 1997, Between Carron and Avon: the Grangemouth area
    since 1600, *Forth Naturalist and Historian*, 20 (1997), 71-91.
10   NAS, CC6/5/20, f. 19 r-v, Testament of Thomas Henderson in Jerah, April
    1687.
11   NAS, RH15/115/1/2, Bundle G, Tack for Foreside and Quarterside of
    Lipney, 1740.
12   GCA, T-SK9/7/13, Tack to Patrick Anderson for Ashentrool, 1743;
    GCA, T-SK9/7/18, Tack to Robert Henderson for Whittetsbank, 1743;
    GCA, T-SK9/7/14, Tack to William Bryce for Cauldhame, 1743; GCA,
    T-SK9/7/15, Tack for 19 years to Richard Henderson for Longcraig, 1742.

THE HISTORY OF FARMING IN MENSTRIE GLEN
13   Menzies Fergusson, R 1905, *Logie: A Parish History*, vol. 2, 169.
14   Menzies Fergusson, R 1905, *Logie: A Parish History*, vol. 1, 306-10.
15   *The Statistical Account of Scotland*, iii, 1792, 287.
16   *Registrum Magni Sigilli Regum Scotorum*, Thomson, J M and others (eds)
    1882-1914, vol. II, 2751.
17   NAS, GD 124/17/188, Tack to Margaret Bonkhill for Jerah, 1534.
18   NAS, GD 124/17/189, Subtack by Margaret Bonkhill to James Porterfield
    and Johne King, 1538.
19   Menzies Fergusson, R 1905, *Logie: A Parish History*, vol. 2, 89.
20   Menzies Fergusson, R 1905, *Logie: A Parish History*, vol. 2, 103; SCA,
    Stirling Protocol Books, B66/1/2 f 3v, B66/1/4 f 39.
21   Menzies Fergusson, R 1905, *Logie: A Parish History*, vol. 2, 169.
22   NAS, RH15/115/1/2, Bundle G, Agreement between McFarlane and Roy,
    1732.
23   NAS, RH15/115/1/1, Bundle H, Agreement between Wright and Andrew
    Roy, 1752.
24   NAS, SC44/59/2, pp. 273-277, Contract of Division and Excambion of
    Ashentrule and Cauldhame, 6th April 1762.
25   Devine, T M 1994, *The Transformation of Rural Scotland: Social Change*
    and the Agrarian Economy, 1660-1815, 65.
26   NAS, RH15/115/4/1, Bundle A, Note of the contents of Loss Farm.
27   NAS, RH15/115/3/1, Bundle A, Rental of the Farms pertaining to James
    Wright of Loss, 1745. This gives rents, the totals of which are: part of
    Loss £194, Foreside of Lipney £105, Backside of Lipney £105, Half of
    Cauldhame £80, Tounhead of Loss £42 3s 8d, Pliverburn £34 10s 4d, and
    Callander of Cauldhame £33 6s 8d.
28   GCA, T-SK9/7/13, Tack to Patrick Anderson for Ashentrool, 1743;
    GCA, T- SK9/7/14, Tack to William Bryce for Cauldhame, 1743; GCA,
    T-SK9/7/15, Tack to Richard Henderson for Longcraig, 1742; GCA, T-
    SK9/7/18, Tack to Robert Henderson for Whittetsbank, 1743.
29   Whyte, I 1979, *Agriculture and Society in Seventeenth-Century Scotland*.
30   Harrison, J G, Between Carron and Avon: the Grangemouth area
    since 1600, *Forth Naturalist and Historian*, 20 (1997), 71-91.
31   Menzies Fergusson, R 1905, *Logie: A Parish History*, vol. 2, 15-16.
32   NAS, CS/S/1/57, Dispute between Holburn of Menstrie and Stirling of
    Keir, 1698.
33   NAS, RH15/115/1/2, Bundle G, Tack to Andrew Roy for Foreside, 1742.
34   NAS, RH15/115/1/2, Bundle G, Tack for Lipney, 1740.
35   NAS, RH15/115/3/1, Bundle D, Account of the Hay and Shearing at Loss,

1753; NAS, RH15/115/1/2, Bundle H, Memorandum.
36   NAS, RH15/115/5/1, Bundle I, Account of the sowing and reaping at
    Loss, 1754 and Account of the Sowing and reaping at Loss, 1755; NAS,
    RH15/115/3/1, Bundle I, Account of the sowing and reaping at Loss,
    1753; NAS, RH15/115/5/1, Bundle K, Account de potatoes, 1754; NAS,
    RH15/115/4/2, Bundle F, Account of the sowing at Loss this year with
    account of the increase, 1758; NAS, RH15/115/5/1, Bundle I, Account
    of the sowing at Loss with account of the number of threaves of Increase,
    1756.
37   NAS, RH15/115/2, Bundle F, Declaration by the Birlaymen about the
    Backside houses, November 25th 1752.
38   GCA, T-SK9/6/7, Tack to Thomas Henderson, 1772.
39   NAS, RH15/115/3/1, Bundle D, Amalgamation of tenancies at Fossachie
    with stipulation that the tenant was not to over lime, 1746.
40   NAS, RH15/115/1/2, Bundle G, Ane Accompt of the rent of Lipnoch,
    1729.
41   GCA, T-SK9/7/13, Tack to Patrick Anderson for Ashentrool, 1743;
    GCA, T-SK9/7/18, Tack to Robert Henderson for Whittetsbank, 1743;
    GCA, T-SK9/7/14, Tack to William Bryce for Cauldhame, 1743; GCA,
    T-SK9/7/15, Tack to Richard Henderson for Longcraig, 1742.
42   NAS, RH15/115/1/2, Bundle G, Tack by Alexander Wright, portioner
    of Ashentrool, to James Burn for Quarterside and Archibald Row for
    Tounhead of Loss, 1701; NAS, RH15/115/5/2, Bundle G, Tack by
    Alexander Wright to Archibald Row, 1704; NAS, RH15/115/4/2, Bundle
    C, Tack by James Wright to Archibald Row for Tounhead, 1715.
43   NAS, RH15/115/4/1, Memorandum about Dividing land with Keir, 1761.
44   NAS, RH15/115/1/2, Bundle G, Tack by James Wright to James Dow,
    1744.
45   NAS, RH15/115/5/1, Book C, Wages for John McGrouther and John
    McGrigor.
46   NAS, RH15/115/5/1, Bundle I, Account of the sowing at Loss with
    account of the number of threaves of Increase, 1756.
47   NAS, RH15/115/1/2, Bundle E, Tack to Patrick Menteith, 1739.
48   NAS, RH15/115/5/1, Bundle K, Articles of the Roup of the Cows *etc.*,
    1759.
49   NAS, RH15/115/5/2, Bundle E, James Wright to Donald Cameron, April
    1760.
50   NAS, RH15/115/1/1, Bundle A, Account of Cattle at Loss, November
    1760.
51   NAS, RH15/115/5/1, Bundle I, Account of the sowing and reaping at Loss,
    1754.
52   NAS, RH15/115/5/2, Bundle F, Account of the persons who carried Lime,
    1755; .NAS, RH15/115/3/1, Bundle K, Account of Expense in improving
    Finshill, 1756.
53   NAS, RH15/115/3/1, Bundle K, Account of Expense in improving
    Finshill, 1755 and 1756.
54   NAS, CC21/13/14 p. 21, Subtack to Wright of Loss for land west of Long
    Calsay, 1767. To be limed and drained before his entry and laid down in
    rye grass and clover; to provide water for pasturing cattle and to be hedged
    and fenced, but Wright is to sow it and labour it for the last three years,
    after using it for pasture for four.
55   NAS, RH15/115/3/1, Bundle D, Purchase of tups, July 1758.
56   NAS, RH15/115/2, Bundle F, Draft Letter by James Wright, November
    16th 1753.
57   NAS, RH15/115/3/1, Bundle K2, Contract between Nicol McAleister and
    James Wright, 1758.
58   NAS, RH15/115/5/2, Bundle E, Memorandum about Dicks measure, 1762.
59   NAS, RH15/115/3/1, Bundle K, Account of Expenses of Building Dykes
    etc., 1757.
60   NAS, SC44/59/2, pp. 273-7, Contract of Division and Excambion of
    Ashentrule and Cauldhame, 6th April 1762.
61   NAS, RH15/115/4/1, Bundle E, Tenants of Fossachie allow under- sowing
    of crop, 1761.
62   NAS, RH15/115/5/2, Legal advice about James Guild's purchase of
    Balquharn and Myreton, Notes about Robert Hoge's tenancy, 1760.
63   NAS, RH15/115/X, Bundle J, Item 6, Letter from McAdam to James
    Wright, March 1763.
64   NAS, RH15/115/3/1, Bundle D, Purchase of tups, July 1758.
65   NAS, RH15/115/3/1, Bundle F, Sheep *etc.* at Fossachie, December 1763;
    NAS, RH15/115/4/1, Bundle A, Account of sheep clipped at Fossachie and
    Lipney, June 1767.
66   NAS, RH15/115/4/2, Bundle A, Letter from Robert Auld to James Wright,
    1761; NAS, RH15/115/3/2, Bundle C, James Wright to Mr Haldane in
    Doune, 1763; NAS, RH15/115/1/1, Bundle A, and NAS, RH15/115/4/2,
    Bundle A, Items regarding lease of Craigton for grazing in 1765; NAS,
    RH15/115/5/2, Bundle G, Item 55, 1766 and 1767; NAS, RH15/ 115/5/2,
    Bundle G, Account of cattle sent to be wintered at Leckie, 1766 and
    1767; NAS, RH15/115/2, Bundle G, Memorandum, February 1766 – '*I*
    have taken 2 Parks at Greenyards of this date to Chrismas next. Note
    that the parks are the Sandy Know and Eassons Park, being all the grass
    enclosures on the north side of the high road from Nether Bannockburn
    to Easter Greenyards'; NAS, RH15/115/2, Bundle G, Item 47, Note of
    21 cattle sent, December 1767 from Greenyards to Fossachie – '*there are*
    6 already there and a bull'; NAS, RH15/115/2, Bundle G, Item 47, Note
    dated February 1767 – '*I have taken from Dr Hey of Greenyards the Park*
    at Greenyards called Easson's Park, where the old Farmhouse stood, that I
    had last year and a small bit east side of ditto from this date to Christmas
    next at £9 7s. Those parks measure about 11 acres'; NAS, RH15/115/2,
    Bundle G, Detail of lease for of Greenyards, 1766-7.

67 *The New Statistical Account of Scotland: Volume VIII Dumbarton – Stirling – Clackmannan*, 1845, Stirlingshire, 215.
68 NAS, RH15/115/3/2, Bundle B, Memorandum about Advertisement of Lipney, 1760.
69 NAS, CC21/6/67, Testament of James Wright, Sale of the Stocking of Fossachie *etc.*, 1770.
70 NAS, RH15/115/3/2, Bundle C, Letter from James Wright to Mr Haldane in Doune, 1763.
71 NAS, RH15/115/4/2, Bundle A, Letter from Robert Auld to James Wright, 1761; NAS, RH15/115/3/2, Bundle C, Letter from James Wright to Mr Haldane in Doune, 1763; NAS, RH15/115/1/1, Bundle A, and NAS, RH15/115/4/ 2, Bundle A, Items regarding lease of Craigton for grazing, 1765.
72 NAS, RH15/115/5/1, Bundle K, Articles of Roup of the Cows, 1758; NAS, RH15/115/5/1, Bundle K, Articles of the Roup of Cows, 1759.
73 NAS, RH15/115/5/2, Bundle G, Item 50, Note of stots and cattle at Fossachie, November 1767.
74 Tipping, R, Waldron, R and Cowley, D C 2001, Pollen Analyses and Historic Landscape Change at Ashentrool, Menstrie Glen, *Forth Naturalist and Historian*, 24 (2001).
75 NAS, CC21/6/61, Testament of James Wright of Loss, 1770.
76 NAS, GD37/209, Elphinstone of Airth papers, 1772; Menzies Fergusson, R 1905, *Logie: A Parish History*, vol. 2, 155.
77 NAS, SC67/49/33, Stirling Sheriff Court Register of Deeds, pp. 331-5, Tack by John Gray to John Robb for Loss, 1782.
78 NAS, GD37/284/13; NAS, GD37/284/18, Tack for Loss, 1803.
79 NAS, GD37/284/23, Tack to Alexander Robb for Loss, 1813.
80 NAS, RHP 20943, Plan of Loss and Lipney, undated.
81 GCA, T-SK20/6, T-SK20/8, T-SK20/9, Keir Estate Rental Books.
82 NAS, RH15/115/2, Bundle D, Obligations by James Mathie, Thomas Hart and Patrick Monteith, 1762.
83 NAS, CC21/13/25, pp. 169-76, Tack for Fossachie to Andrew Roy, 1807.
84 SCA, Census for 1841, Logie Parish, Stirlingshire, District 3 – includes Loss and Cauldhame.
85 SCA, Census for 1841, Logie Parish, Stirlingshire, District 3 – includes Loss and Cauldhame.
86 Ordnance Survey Name Book of the Part of the Parish of Logie in the County of Stirling, No. 20 (1858-61); SCA, Census for 1851, Logie Parish, Stirlingshire, District 3.
87 SCA, SC4/3/1, Valuation Roll for Stirlingshire, 1831; SCA, SC4/3/2, Valuation Roll for Stirlingshire, 1855-6.
88 SCA, Census for 1861, Logie parish, Stirlingshire, District 9 – includes Lipney; District 10 – includes Jerah House and Jerah Cottage.
89 Elliott, B J 1993, Agriculture, in Corbett, L, Dix, N J, Bryant, D M, McLusky, D, Elliott, B J and Tranter, N, *Central Scotland: Land – Wildlife – People,* Forth Naturalist and Historian, 127.
90 *The Third Statistical Account of Scotland: The counties of Stirling and Clackmannan*, 1966, 466.

THE SETTLEMENTS

91 NAS, GD24/1/319, Printed Depositions of Witnesses, 1699, p. 3, Evidence of John Sharp; p. 5, Evidence of William Drysdale; p. 6, Evidence of John Dickie; p. 12, Evidence of John Somervel; p. 15, Evidence of Magnus Gib; p. 17, Evidence of Thomas Guild; NAS, GD24/1/319, Small bundle, letter from Rollo, 1659; NAS, GD24/1/ 319, Small bundle, Submission and meeting; NAS, GD24/1/319, Instrument of Interruption, 1632.
92 NAS, RH15/115/4/1, Bundle E, Tenants of Fossachie to allow undersowing of crop, 1761; Menzies Fergusson, R 1905, *Logie: A Parish History*, vol. 2, 82.
93 Fenton, A and Walker, B 1981, *The Rural Architecture of Scotland*, 75.
94 NAS, RH15/115/1/2, Bundle G, Account of expenses, 1730.
95 Gailey, R A 1962, The Peasant Houses of the South-west Highland of Scotland: Distribution, Parallels and Evolution, *Gwerin*, 3 no. 5 (1962), 233.
96 NAS, RH15/115/2, Bundle F, Declaration by the Birlaymen about the Backside houses, November 25th 1752.
97 NAS, RH15/115/2, Bundle G, Repairs to the Backside Houses, 1753.
98 NAS, RH15/115/1/2, Bundle G, Repairs to Foreside of Lipney, 24th February 1730.
99 NAS, RH15/115/1/2, Bundle G, Agreement between Donald McFarlane and Andrew Roy, 1760.
100 Menzies Fergusson, R 1905, *Logie: A Parish History*, vol. 2, 14.
101 NAS, RH15/115/3/1, Bundle K, Account between Loss and Robert Stirling, 1756.
102 NAS, RH15/115/3/1, Bundle K, Account of Tounhead house, 1756.
103 NAS, RH15/115/3/1, Bundle K, Account of expenses in repairing Tounhead house for a weaver, 1757.
104 NAS, RH15/115/3/1, Bundle K2, Patrick Stirling's Account, 1757.
105 NAS, RH15/115/3/1, Bundle B, Account of expense in repairing Tounhead house for a smith, 1762.
106 NAS, RH15/115/1/2, Bundle G, Repairs to Foreside of Lipney, 24th February 1730.
107 NAS, RH15/115/4/2, Bundle C, Tack to Robert Duncanson, 7th February 1763.
108 NLS, James Stobie 1783, The Counties of Perth and Clackmannan.
109 Menzies Fergusson, R 1905, *Logie: A Parish History*, vol. 2, 155.
110 NAS, RH15/115/5/2, Bundle D, Papers relating to Loss, 1744-5.
111 NAS, RH15/115/1/2, Tack to James Dow, 1744.
112 NAS, RH15/115/2, Bundle F, Draft letters by James Wright, 1752 and 1753.
113 NAS, RH15/115/2, Bundle J, Summary account for work at Loss, 1750-52.
114 NAS, RH15/115/3/1, Bundle K, Work at Loss, 1753-4.
115 RCAHMS 1963, *Stirlingshire: An Inventory of Ancient Monuments*, 46.
116 NAS, SC67/49/27, Stirling Sheriff Court Register of Deeds, pp. 215-19, Post-nuptial marriage contract, 1755.
117 NAS, SC67/49/33, Stirling Sheriff Court Register of Deeds, pp. 331-5, Tack by John Gray to John Robb for Loss, 1782.
118 SCA, Census for 1841, Logie Parish, Stirlingshire, District 3 – includes Loss and Cauldhame.
119 Ordnance Survey Name Book of the Part of the Parish of Logie in the County of Stirling, No. 20 (1858-61).
120 2nd edition of the OS 6-inch map, Stirlingshire 1909, sheets x and xi.
121 NAS, GD37/284/23, Tack to Alexander Robb for Loss, 1813.
122 1st edition of the OS 6-inch map, Perthshire and Clackmannanshire 1865-6, sheet cxxxiii; Stirlingshire 1865-6, sheets x and xi.
123 SCA, Uncatalogued Item; Register of Plans Approved by the Local Authority, Western Stirlingshire, 1939-1955.
124 NLS, James Stobie 1783, The Counties of Perth and Clackmannan. Also known as Wester Jerah.
125 1st edition of the OS 6-inch map, Perthshire and Clackmannanshire 1865-6, sheet cxxxiii; Stirlingshire 1865-6, sheets x and xi.
126 Ordnance Survey Name Book of the Part of the Parish of Logie in the County of Stirling, No. 20, (1858-61).
127 3rd edition of the OS 6-inch map, Stirlingshire 1951, (NS) sheet xi N.E.; Perthshire 1951, sheets cxxxii and cxxxiii.
128 1st edition of the OS 6-inch map, Perthshire and Clackmannanshire 1865-6, sheet cxxxiii; Stirlingshire 1865-6, sheets x and xi.
129 2nd edition of the OS 6-inch map, Stirlingshire 1909, sheets x and xi.

THE ARCHAEOLOGY OF THE LANDSCAPE

130 NAS, RH15/115/1/2, Bundle G, Tack to Donald McFarlane and Andrew Roy, 1730.
131 NAS, RH15/115/1/2, Bundle G, Tack by James Wright to Andrew Roy for Foreside and Quarterside and half the hill, 1740; NAS, RH15/115/1/2, Bundle G, Tack by James Wright to James McFarlane for Backside, 1740.
132 NAS, RH15/115/1/2, Bundle G, Tacks to Andrew Roy for Foreside of Lipney, and Robert Dow for Backside of Lipney, 1752.
133 NAS, RH15/115/1/2, Bundle G, Tack by James Wright to James McFarlane, 1740.
134 NAS, RH15/115/1/2, Bundle G, Tack by James Wright to Andrew Roy for Foreside and Quarterside and half the hill for 13 years, 1740; NAS, RH15/115/1/2, Bundle G, Tack by James Wright to James McFarlane for Backside, 1740.
135 NAS, RHP 20943, Plan of Loss and Lipney, undated.
136 1st edition of the OS 6-inch map, Perthshire and Clackmannanshire 1865-6, sheet cxxxiii; Stirlingshire 1865-6, sheets x and xi.
137 Dixon, P J 1994, Field systems, Rig and Other Cultivation Remains in Scotland: The Field Evidence, in Foster, S and Smout, T C (eds) 1994, *The History of Soils and Field Systems*, 38.
138 NAS, RH15/115/3/1, Bundle K, Account of Expense in improving Finshill, 1755 and 1756.
139 Fenton, A 1976, *Scottish Country Life*, 38- 43.
140 1st edition of the OS 6-inch map, Perthshire and Clackmannanshire 1865-6, sheet cxxxiii; Stirlingshire 1865-6, sheets x and xi.
141 NAS, RH15/115/1/2, Bundle G, Tack by James Wright to Andrew Roy.
142 Dickie, D M 1976, Cultivation terraces along the Ochil escarpment, a preliminary survey, *Forth Naturalist and Historian*, 1 (1976), 122-39.
143 NAS, RH15/115/4/2, Bundle C, Tack by James Wright to Archibald Row for Tounhead, 1715.
144 NAS, RH15/115/1/2, Bundle G, Agreement between Donald McFarlane and Andrew Roy, 1732.
145 NAS, RH15/115/1/2, Bundle G, Tack by James Wright to Andrew Roy for Foreside and Quarterside of Lipney, 1740.
146 NAS, RH15/115/1/2, Tack by James Wright to Dow, 1752.
147 NAS, RH15/115/4/2, Bundle F, Account of sowing of Loss, 1758.
148 NAS, RH15/115/1/2, Bundle G, Tack by James Wright to James MacFarlane for Backside, 1740.
149 NAS, RH15/115/5/1, Bundle I, Account of the sowing at Loss with account of the number of threaves of Increase, 1756.
150 NAS, RH15/115/3/1, Bundle K, Account of Expenses of Building Dykes *etc.*, 1757.
151 NAS, RH15/115/3/1, Bundle K2, Contract between Nicol McAleister and James Wright, 1758.
152 NAS, RH15/115/3/1, Bundle K2, Contract between Nicol McAleister and James Wright, 1758.
153 NAS, RH15/115/2, Bundle E, Memorandum about Dicks measure, 1762.
154 NAS, RH15/115/3/1, Bundle H, Park Dike at Broomhill, 1764.
155 NAS, RH15/115/3/2, Bundle D, Memorandum de Fossachy begun 2nd Jan 1761, Item 41, for payments for dykes, paling *etc.* not noted here.
156 NAS, SC67/49/33, pp. 331-517, Tack by John Gray to John Robb for Loss, 1782.
157 NAS, CC21/13/25, pp. 169-176, Tack for Fossachie, 1808.
158 1st edition of the OS 6-inch map, Perthshire and Clackmannanshire 1865-6, sheet cxxxiii; Stirlingshire 1865-6, sheets x and xi.
159 Ward, T 1998, *Glenochar Bastle House and Fermtoun*, Biggar Museum Trust.

160 NAS, RH15/115/1/2, Marches between the proper lands of Fossowye, pertaining to the Laird of Knockhill and ye lands of Blairlogie, pertaining to the Laird of Blair. This is an 18th century copy of the original document of 1590, and includes a very roughly redrawn plan.

161 NAS, RH15/115/1/1, Bundle F, Scroll contract of agreement about Mines, 1717.

162 NAS, RH15/115/1/1, Bundle F, Agreement about Mines, 1754.

163 NAS, CC6/12/10, p. 537, Tack for Parsonleys, 1732.

164 NAS, RH15/115/1/1, Bundle A, Letter from Patrick Linton to James Wright of Loss, 10th May 1732.

165 NAS, RH15/115/5/2, Bundle E, Correspondence between James Wright and Stirling of Keir, January 1761; NAS, RH15/115/4/1, Bundle D, Memorandum about Dividing land with Keir, 1761.

166 NAS, SC44/59/2, pp. 273-7, Contract of Division and Excambion of Ashentrule and Cauldhame, 6th April 1762.

167 NAS, RH15/115/2, Bundle E, Memorandum about dykes, 1762; NAS, RH15/115/3/1, Bundle H, Ditch between Captain Haldane and Keir, 1763; NAS, RH15/115/5/1, Book 2, Building about Tounhead and March-dyke between Keir and Loss, 1763; NAS, RH15/115/1/2, Bundle C, Memorandum about Dykes between Keir and Loss, 1764; NAS, RH15/115/2, Bundle E, Account of Ditch at Backside, June 18th 1763.

168 NAS, RH15/115/1/2, Bundle C, About thorns delivered, 1764; NAS, RH15/115/3/1, Bundle I, About thorns, 1765.

169 NAS, RH1/115/5/1, Bundle K, Draft tack by Haldane to James Wright, 1761.

170 NAS, RH15/115/4/2, Bundle E, March-dyke between Ashentrool and Lipney, 1768.

171 NAS, SC64/55/7, Bundle 1807, Contract of Excambion between George Abercromby and James Guild, 1768.

172 NAS, RH15/115/5/2, Bundle 7, and NAS, RH15/115/4/1, Bundle A, Proposals to straighten the Auld Wharry Burn, 1761.

173 NAS, GD37/284/23, Tack for Loss to Alexander Robb, 1813.

174 Callander, R 1988, Sheep Houses in Midlothian County, *Vernacular Building*, 12 (1998), 3-13.

175 Donaldson, J 1697, *Husbandry Anatomised*, 99.

176 NAS, SC44/59/2, pp. 273-7, Contract of Division and Excambion of Ashentrule and Cauldhame, 6th April 1762.

177 NAS, RH15/115/5/2, Bundle D, Buildings at Loss, 1744 and 1745.

178 NAS, RH15/115/1/2, Bundle H, Memorandum, September 1762.

179 NAS, RH15/115/1/2, Bundle G, Repairs to Foreside of Lipney, 24th February 1730.

180 NAS, RH15/115/3, Bundle F, Declaration by the Birlaymen about the Backside houses, November 25th 1752.

181 NAS, RH15/115/3/1, Account, George Tailor and Brown, 1753.

182 NAS, SC64/55/1, Bundle for 1714, Contract, Dundas of Manor with Daniel Peck of London and John Adair, to exploit the Logie mines, 1696. Dundas was to drain the old mines as a preliminary.

183 NAS, RH15/115/1, Bundle F, Receipt by Howison, 1726.

184 NAS, RH15/115/1, Bundle F, A list of damnified ground, June 1729.

185 NAS, RH15/115/1/1, Bundle F, Receipt by Alexander Watt, May 1735.

186 NAS, RH15/115/1/1, Bundle F, Mr Sincler to James Wright, 1754, Copy of the Lease of the Mines of Loss, 1753 and 1754.

187 NAS, RH15/115/1/1, Bundle F, Instrument of Protest, James Wright against Weston, 1761.

188 NAS, RH15/115/1/1, Bundle F, Scroll contract, 1760.

189 NAS, RH15/115/1/1, Bundle F, Draft letter to Mr Weston and Mr Freebairn, 1769.

190 NAS, RH15/115/1/1, Bundle F, Instrument of Protest, James Wright against Weston, 1761.

191 NAS, RH15/115/1/1, Bundle F, Letter from James Stephens to James Wright, 18th March 1761.

192 NAS, RH15/115/4/2, Bundle F, Letter from Patten to James Wright, December 1761; NAS, RH15/115/5/1, Bundle E, Letter from James Stephens to James Wright, 1761; NAS, RH15/115/5/2, Bundle G, Letter from Thomas Paton to James Wright, December 1762.

193 NAS, RH15/115/3/2, Bundle D, Letter from Patten to James Wright, 1762; NAS, RH15/115/5/2, Bundle G, December 1762.

194 NAS, RH15/115/3/2, Bundle D, Letter from Richardson to James Wright, 9th May 1763.

195 Robertson, T, Simpson, J B and Anderson, J G C 1949, *The Limestones of Scotland*, 85.

CONCLUSIONS

196 Devine, T M 1994, *The Transformation of Rural Scotland: Social Change and the Agrarian Economy, 1660-1815*, 64-5.

197 Devine, T M 1994, *The Transformation of Rural Scotland: Social Change and the Agrarian Economy, 1660-1815*, 65.

198 RCAHMS 1997, *Eastern Dumfriesshire: an archaeological landscape*, 36-9, 89-91.

JAMES WRIGHT OF LOSS: 1730-69

199 NLS, MS3190, Balhaldie Papers, Old Compt Book, end papers: '*James Wright was born upon the eleventh day of December 1730 about 8 a cloak at night being Friday*'.

200 Menzies Fergusson, R 1905, *Logie: A Parish History*, vol. 2, 154; Young, R T 1932, The Wrights of Loss: An Ochil Family, *Transactions of the Stirling Field and Archaeological Society*, 52 (1932), 126. All these properties were acquired by marriage. Menzies Fergusson conflates James Wright, the father, with 'our' James.

201 NAS, RH15/115/3/1, Bundle E, Letter from James Wright to Thomas Duthie '*I must be a syrurgeon or merchant. I will not do for a writer*' (We are grateful to Rosemary Cowtan for this reference); Young, R T 1932, The Wrights of Loss: An Ochil Family, *Transactions of the Stirling Field and Archaeological Society*, 52 (1932), 129-130.

202 NAS, RH15/115/4/1, Bundle B, Letter from Jacobina Drummond to James Wright, 12th June 1749.

203 NAS, RH15/115/1/1, Bundle B, Invitations to baptism of child, Margaret, 23rd July 1751, Drummond to James Wright, Letter of congratulation on birth, 2nd October 1751; Young, R T 1932, The Wrights of Loss: An Ochil Family, *Transactions of the Stirling Field and Archaeological Society*, 52 (1932), 133.

204 NAS, RH15/115/3/2, Bundle E, Thomas Glass to James Wright, 15th April 1765; Ronald, J 1906, *The story of Argyle Lodging*, 139.

205 NAS, RH15/115/3/2, Bundle E, Letter Thomas Glass to James Wright, 15th April 1765; NLS, Add Mss 82.4.8 55r –55v, Oliphant of Gask Papers, Copy letter Wm McKillop to Laurence Oliphant of Condie, 28th November 1769; Ronald, J 1906, *The story of Argyle Lodging*, Stirling, 139.

206 NAS, RH15/115/5/1, Bundle C, Alpine Drummond's wages.

207 NAS, RH15/115/3/2, Bundle A, Letters from Mr Innes, 1761.

208 NAS, RH15/115/2, Bundles B, C and D, Letters from Mr Buchanan, 1768.

209 NAS, RH15/115/3/2, Bundle B, Proposals for West Indian plantation.

210 NAS, RH15/115/5/2, Bundle G, To the Gentlemen of South and North Uist *etc.*, 1763; NAS, RH15/115/1/2, Bundle D, Gaelic phrases.

211 NAS, RH15/115/2, Bundle F, Letter from Jacobina Drummond to James Wright, July 1763.

212 NAS, RH15/115/4/1, Bundle B, Letter from Jacobina Drummond to James Wright, 15th June 1764.

213 NAS, RH15/115/3/2, Bundle E, Letter from D. Drummond to James Wright, 9th September 1764.

214 NAS, RH15/115/3/1, Bundle C; NAS, RH15/115/3/2, Bundle E, L. Drummond to James Wright, 9th September 1768, February 1768; NAS, RH15/115/5/1, Bundle K, Letters from L. Drummond, 1757.

215 NAS, RH15/115/3/2, Bundle E, Letter from Wright of Glinns to James Wright about a servant in trouble for smuggling, 1761.

216 NAS, RH15/115/5/1, Bundle K, Remarks from Mr Dalrymple, 1762.

217 NAS, RH15/115/1/1, Bundle G, Letter from James McAdam to James Wright, 10th May 1763.

218 Young, R T 1932, The Wrights of Loss: An Ochil Family, *Transactions of the Stirling Field and Archaeological Society*, 52 (1932), 144-5.

219 NAS, RH15/115/3/2, Bundle D, Various letters from the Bruces of Kennet, Abercrombie of Tulliebody, and Mrs Haldane of Gleneagles to James Wright.

220 NAS, RH15/115/4/2, Bundle A, Letter from Mr Auld to James Wright, 1767.

221 NAS, RH15/115/3/2, Bundle D, Invitation and Tickets; Young, R T 1932, The Wrights of Loss: An Ochil Family, *Transactions of the Stirling Field and Archaeological Society*, 52 (1932), 142-5.

222 NAS, RH15/115/5/2, Bundle G, Cameron genealogy; NAS, RH15/115/3/2, Bundle C, Letter from Ewan Cameron to James Wright, December 1762.

223 NAS, RH15/115/2, Bundle F, James Wright to Balhaldie, 28th May 1752; Young, R T 1932, The Wrights of Loss: An Ochil Family, *Transactions of the Stirling Field and Archaeological Society*, 52 (1932), 133.

224 NAS, RH15/115/3/2, Bundle B, Advertisement of Lipney, 1760.

225 NAS, RH15/115/2, Bundle D, Letter to Mrs Campbell, November 1756.

226 NAS, RH15/115/2, Bundle D, 9th November 1756.

227 NAS, RH15/115/3/2, Bundle C, James Fergus to James Wright, 1759.

228 NAS, RH15/115/3/2, Bundle E, Capt. Barclay Maitland to James Wright regarding Division of Tillicoultry, *c.* 1769.

GLOSSARY OF TERMS

229 SND 1941-76, *The Scottish National Dictionary*, Grant, W and Murison, D A (eds), Edinburgh; Zupko, R E 1985, *A dictionary of weights and measures for the British Isles*, American Philospohical Society, Philadelphia.

REFERENCES

Callander, R 1988
Sheep Houses in Midlothian County
Vernacular Building, 12, 3-13
Scottish Vernacular Buildings Working Group, Edinburgh

Corbett, L, Dix, N J, Bryant, D M, McLusky, D, Elliott, B J and Tranter, N 1993
Central Scotland: Land – Wildlife – People
Forth Naturalist and Historian, Stirling

Devine, T M 1994
The Transformation of Rural Scotland: Social Change and the Agrarian Economy, 1660-1815
Edinburgh

Dickie, D M 1976
Cultivation terraces along the Ochil escarpment, a preliminary survey
Forth Naturalist and Historian, 1 (1976), 122-39

Dixon, P J 1994
Field systems, Rig and Other Cultivation Remains in Scotland: The Field Evidence in Foster, S and Smout, T C (eds) 1994, 26-52

Donaldson, J 1697
Husbandry Anatomised
Edinburgh

Elliott, B J 1993
Agriculture
in Corbett, L *et al.* 1993, 125-40

Fenton, A 1976
Scottish Country Life
Edinburgh

Fenton, A and Walker, B 1981
The Rural Architecture of Scotland
Edinburgh

Foster, S and Smout, T C (eds) 1994
The History of Soils and Field Systems
Aberdeen

Gailey, R A 1962
The Peasant Houses of the South-west Highland of Scotland: Distribution, Parallels and Evolution
Gwerin, 3, no. 5, 227-42

Harrison, J G 1997
Between Carron and Avon: the Grangemouth area since 1600
Forth Naturalist and Historian, 20, 71-91

Menzies Fergusson, R 1905
Logie: A Parish History
Paisley

NSA 1845
The New Statistical Account of Scotland: VIII Dumbarton – Stirling – Clackmannan
Edinburgh

Reg. Mag. Sig.
Registrum Magni Sigilli Regum Scotorum
Thomson, J M and others (eds) 1882-1914
Edinburgh

RCAHMS
Royal Commission on the Ancient and Historical Monuments of Scotland

RCAHMS 1963
Stirlingshire: An Inventory of Ancient Monuments
Edinburgh

RCAHMS 1997
Eastern Dumfriesshire: an archaeological landscape
Edinburgh

Robertson, T, Simpson, J B and Anderson, J G C 1949
The Limestones of Scotland
Edinburgh

Ronald, J 1906
The story of Argyle Lodging
Stirling

SND 1941-76
The Scottish National Dictionary
Grant, W and Murison, D A (eds)
Edinburgh

Stat. Acct. 1792
The Statistical Account of Scotland, III
Sinclair, J (ed.)
Edinburgh

Tipping, R, Waldron, R and Cowley, D C 2001
Pollen Analyses and Historic Landscape Change at Ashentrool, Menstrie Glen
Forth Naturalist and Historian, 24

TSA 1966
The Third Statistical Account of Scotland: The counties of Stirling and Clackmannan
Gordon, T C (ed.)
Glasgow

Ward, T 1998
Glenochar Bastle House and Fermtoun
Biggar Museum Trust

Watson, A 1995
The Ochils: Placenames, History, Tradition
Perth and Kinross District Libraries

Whyte, I 1979
Agriculture and Society in Seventeenth-Century Scotland
Edinburgh

Young, R T 1932
The Wrights of Loss: An Ochil Family
Transactions of the Stirling Field and Archaeological Society, 52, 125-149

Zupko, R E 1985
A dictionary of weights and measures for the British Isles
American Philospohical Society, Philadelphia

GLOSSARY OF TERMS

This glossary provides short definitions for the less common terms used in the text and attempts to convey the local essence of words where relevant. It draws on The Scottish National Dictionary and Zupko.[229]

Aitseed: seed oats.
Arrises: sharp edges at the meeting of two surfaces, in this case the front and sides of the fireplace.
Bear/bere: a hardy four-rowed variety of barley.
Bigging: building or building work.
Birlaymen: tenants acting as judges of customary law on the estate, particularly of the value of damage or costs of repairs.
Bol/Boll: a dry measure of grain = 85 pints for wheat, peas, beans, rye; = 124 pints for barley, oats, malt.
Bucht: a pen or small fold for sheep, e.g. for milking or clipping.
Byre: a cow shed or cow house.
Caber: a rafter.
Chalder: a measurement of grain (8 bolls).
Contraverted: disputed.
Couple: synonymous with cruck in the context of the 18th century documents in Menstrie Glen.
Cruck: a curved timber supporting roof, and springing from the ground or within the wall thickness. Arranged in pairs spaced regularly along a building to take the weight of the roof.
Decreet: a court judgement, in this case a formal legal definition of new boundaries.
Ell: a linear measurement of about 37 inches (94 cm).
Emparkment: enclosed ground around a grand house, put over to grass and planted with decorative trees, sometimes in avenues or clumps.
Excambion: an exchange of land.
Fall: a linear measurement of 6 ells (5.6 m).
Fank: a sheepfold.
Fauld: a fold or pen – can be a part of outfield brought into temporary cultivation having had cattle or sheep folded on it, i.e. tathing.
Firlot: a dry measure of grain = about 1/4 of a boll.
Feal: turf.
Furr: a furrow or ditch – separating one rig from another.
Gavel: a gable end, or the triangular upper part of an end wall.
Hallan: a partition between living room and byre, or between door and fireplace.
Head-dyke: a dyke, usually earthen, which divided the tenants' land, including arable, meadow and pasture, below the dyke from the common pastures above.
Hogg: a sheep of 6 to 12 months old.
Imprimis: in the first place.
Kine: cows.
Lambas/Lammas: 1st August, feast of the first fruits.
Ley: fallow arable sown with grass.
Loaning: a cattle path to pasture, or a lane.
Lum: a chimney, wide wooden canopy suspended over fire to serve as a smoke vent.
Lynchet: a break of slope caused by soil movement, usually through ploughing. Can form at the bottom of a field or rig through soil build-up or at the top through erosion.
Mainsing: the home farm of an estate, usually worked by the proprietor but sometimes leased.
March-dyke: a boundary wall separating one farm from another.
Martinmas: 11th November, feast of St Martin.
Midden: a dung heap.
Muir: a moor.
Nolt: young cattle.
Paling/pealing: a wooden fence, made of stakes.

Pan: a horizontal roof member fixed to the couples.
Pan and roof: a common expression referring to the whole roof.
Park: an area of enclosed ground usually for grazing.
Peck: a dry measure of grain = about 1/4 of a firlot.
Poinfold: a fold for confining stray animals.
Portioner: the proprietor of a small estate, once part of a larger holding.
Rig: a strip of ploughed ground, bounded by a furrow on either side.
Roup: an auction.
Rumeling siver: an underground drain, filled at its base with stone.
Sheep-house: a building for sheltering sheep overnight.
Shieling-hut: a small building for shelter and storage during summer pasturage of livestock.
Sitt house: a dwelling house, especially on a farm.
Stackyard: a yard for stacks of hay and unthreshed crop.
Steading: farm buildings.
Stouk: a set of corn sheaves.
Stot: a young ox or steer.
Tack: a lease of property, a tenancy.
Tathing: folding of beasts on future arable to provide the benefit of manure.
Teind: a tithe, a tenth part.
Thak: thatch.
Threave: generally two stouks of ten sheaves each.
Tirr: to strip or pull down.
Tirrings: what has been stripped – e.g. in these cases the old thatch.
Tofts: small pieces of land enclosed for cultivation, i.e. for cabbages, attached to a house.
Tup: a ram.
Wedder: a wether, which is a castrated male sheep bred for its fleece and mutton.